AF800000

What Christians should know about the Qur'an and Muhammad

Baher Foad

Evidence from the Qur'an & tradition of Prophet Muhammad

What Christians should know about the Qur'an and Muhammad

TATE PUBLISHING
AND ENTERPRISES, LLC

What Christians should know about the Qur'an and Muhammad

Published by Tate Publishing & Enterprises, LLC
127 E. Trade Center Terrace | Mustang, Oklahoma 73064 USA
1.888.361.9473 | www.tatepublishing.com

Tate Publishing is committed to excellence in the publishing industry. The company reflects the philosophy established by the founders, based on Psalm 68:11,
"The Lord gave the word and great was the company of those who published it."

Cover design by Bill Francis Peralta
Interior design by Shieldon Alcasid

Published in the United States of America

ISBN: 978-1-68164-464-6
1. Religion / Islam / Koran & Sacred Writings
2. Religion / Islam / General
15.07.23

Contents

Introduction

Many Christians do not know what the Qur'an stands for or what its message is and teachings. Some have been told that Muhammad wrote the Qur'an and that the Qur'an is not a divine book.

Many Christians have heard about Muhammad, but not from a Muslim perspective. Some have been told that he was a worrier who waged wars and wanted to force Islam on Christians. They have heard that he married many wives.

This book is intended for Christians who want to learn about the Qur'an and Muhammad from a Muslim perspective. It discusses the Qur'an and its teachings and how the life of Muhammad is closely related to the Qur'an. It is documented with verses from the Qur'an and from the sayings of Muhammad.

The book is divided into two parts. The first part explores the Qur'an: what is it, who wrote it, and how it was preserved. It gives the evidence of the book being an authentic divine revelation and discusses its message and guidelines. It also compares faith and morality in the Qur'an and the New Testament, and outlines basic differences between the two books. Then it clears some misconceptions about the Qur'an.

The second part explores the life of Muhammad and the lessons we can learn from his character and behavior, and the various stages of his life. Then it discusses his sayings and tradition, and what he represents to Muslims and clears some misconceptions about him.

PART I

THE QUR'AN

1

What Is the Qur'an? Who Wrote it?

To Muslims, the Qur'an is the literal word of God that He inspired to Prophet Muhammad peace be upon him. Muhammad did *not* write the Qur'an, for he was illiterate and could not read or write. The Qur'an came down interrupted over twenty-three years, and the last verses were revealed shortly before the death of Muhammad.

The Qur'an states,

كِتَٰبٌ أَنزَلْنَٰهُ إِلَيْكَ لِتُخْرِجَ ٱلنَّاسَ مِنَ ٱلظُّلُمَٰتِ إِلَى ٱلنُّورِ بِإِذْنِ رَبِّهِمْ إِلَىٰ صِرَٰطِ
ٱلْعَزِيزِ ٱلْحَمِيدِ ﴿١﴾

> A Book that We sent to you, in order that you may lead out mankind from the depths of darkness into the light, by the leave of their Lord, to the way of Him Exalted in power, worthy of praise. (Ibrahim [Prophet Abraham] 14: 1)

The Qur'an was revealed in Arabic because Muhammad, God's last messenger, was an Arab. God sends His divine revelations to His prophets and messengers in the language of their own people. The prophet explains God's message and applies it in his character and behavior and becomes an example to follow.

﴿ وَمَآ أَرْسَلْنَا مِن رَّسُولٍ إِلَّا بِلِسَانِ قَوْمِهِۦ لِيُبَيِّنَ لَهُمْ

> We sent not a messenger except to teach in the language of his own people. (Ibrahim [Prophet Abraham] 14: 4)

The Qur'an came down gradually, and in stages, over twenty-three years in order to strengthen the heart of the prophet and his companions, and to answer questions and solve problems that faced them. The Qur'an states,

﴿ وَقَالَ ٱلَّذِينَ كَفَرُوا۟ لَوْلَا نُزِّلَ عَلَيْهِ ٱلْقُرْءَانُ جُمْلَةً وَٰحِدَةً ۚ كَذَٰلِكَ لِنُثَبِّتَ بِهِۦ فُؤَادَكَ ۖ وَرَتَّلْنَٰهُ
تَرْتِيلًا ﴿٣٢﴾ وَلَا يَأْتُونَكَ بِمَثَلٍ إِلَّا جِئْنَٰكَ بِٱلْحَقِّ وَأَحْسَنَ تَفْسِيرًا ﴿٣٣﴾ ﴾

> Those who reject faith say: "Why is not the Qur'an revealed to him all at once?
>
> Thus it was revealed that We may strengthen your heart thereby, and We have rehearsed it to you in slow, well-arranged stages, gradually. And no question do they bring to you but We reveal to you

the truth and best explanation." (Al-Furqan [The Criterion] 25:32–33)

If the Qur'an came all at once, it would have been impossible for the prophet and his companions to read it, memorize it, or apply its message in their behavior. Therefore, the gradual revelation of the Qur'an over many years is a mercy and blessing from God.

How Was the Qur'an Preserved?

As soon as Prophet Muhammad (PBUH) received the divine revelation, he ordered the Qur'an to be preserved in two ways: oral and written. A group of his companions were charged with memorizing the Qur'anic verses being revealed. Another group was charged with writing these Qur'anic verses on material available at the time. Muslims recite the Qur'an in their five daily prayers. Therefore, it is not difficult to memorize few verses if they are recited daily in prayer.

Thus the Qur'an was safeguarded from alteration. The Qur'an states that God promised to safeguard His message:

﴿ إِنَّا نَحْنُ نَزَّلْنَا ٱلذِّكْرَ وَإِنَّا لَهُۥ لَحَٰفِظُونَ ﴾

> We have, without doubt, sent down the message, and We will assuredly guard it. (Al-Hijr [Rocky Tracts] 15:9)

During the rule of Abu Bakr, the first righteous caliph, the written Qur'an was collected and was compared to the oral Qur'an preserved in the hearts of the prophet's companions. Nothing was accepted as a Qur'an unless it confirmed to the recitation of the prophet and witnesses swore that it was the true Qur'an. At the time of Uthman, the third righteous caliph, the Qur'an was written in one version to facilitate its reading.

What is the proof that the Qur'an is a revelation from God and not the work of a human being?

1. Evidence from the Qur'an

    a. The Qur'an is clear and logical. It addresses our hearts and minds.

    b. None of the verses in the Qur'an have been proven wrong.

    c. There is no contradiction in the Qur'an. Rather, its verses complete and complement one another.

2. Evidence from the life of Muhammad (PBUH)

    a. Muhammad was illiterate: he could not read nor write.

    b. No one could produce such a Qur'an.

The Qur'an Is Clear and Logical

The Qur'an answers questions in a clear way that makes sense. Those who reject faith argue about the resurrection: how can they be raised up from the dead and given life again? The Qur'an gives the answer in two ways: 1) God, who gave life to begin with, is capable of giving life again after you die. 2) Look at the dead earth, how it is stirred to life again. God, who revives the dead earth, is surely capable of resurrecting the dead.

﴿أَوَلَمْ يَرَ ٱلْإِنسَٰنُ أَنَّا خَلَقْنَٰهُ مِن نُّطْفَةٍ فَإِذَا هُوَ خَصِيمٌ مُّبِينٌ ﴿٧٧﴾ وَضَرَبَ لَنَا مَثَلًا وَنَسِىَ خَلْقَهُۥ
قَالَ مَن يُحْىِ ٱلْعِظَٰمَ وَهِىَ رَمِيمٌ ﴿٧٨﴾ قُلْ يُحْيِيهَا ٱلَّذِىٓ أَنشَأَهَآ أَوَّلَ مَرَّةٍ وَهُوَ بِكُلِّ خَلْقٍ عَلِيمٌ
﴿٧٩﴾﴾

> Does not man see that it is We who created him from sperm, yet he stands as an open adversary. And he makes comparisons for us, and forgets his own creation, he says: "Who can give life to dry and decomposed bones?" Say: "He will give them life who created them for the first time, for He fully knows all creation. (Ya Sin 36:77–79)

﴿وَمِنْ ءَايَٰتِهِۦٓ أَنَّكَ تَرَى ٱلْأَرْضَ خَٰشِعَةً فَإِذَآ أَنزَلْنَا عَلَيْهَا ٱلْمَآءَ ٱهْتَزَّتْ وَرَبَتْ إِنَّ ٱلَّذِىٓ أَحْيَاهَا
لَمُحْىِ ٱلْمَوْتَىٰٓ إِنَّهُۥ عَلَىٰ كُلِّ شَىْءٍ قَدِيرٌ ﴿٣٩﴾﴾

> And among His signs is that you see the earth humble, but when We send down rain to it, it is

> stirred to life and yields increase. Truly He who gives life to the dead earth can surely give life to those who are dead, for He has power over all things. (Fussilat [Explained in Detail]) 41:39)

The righteous are not treated in the same way as the wicked. Every soul is rewarded or punished according to its deeds, no one is wronged. There is justice and accountability

﴿ أَمْ نَجْعَلُ ٱلَّذِينَ ءَامَنُوا۟ وَعَمِلُوا۟ ٱلصَّٰلِحَٰتِ كَٱلْمُفْسِدِينَ فِى ٱلْأَرْضِ أَمْ نَجْعَلُ ٱلْمُتَّقِينَ كَٱلْفُجَّارِ
﴿٢٨﴾ ﴾

> Shall We treat those who believe and work deeds of righteousness, the same as those who do mischief on earth? Shall We treat those who guard against evil, the same as those who turn aside from the right? (Sa'D 38:28)

﴿ أَمْ حَسِبَ ٱلَّذِينَ ٱجْتَرَحُوا۟ ٱلسَّيِّـَٔاتِ أَن نَّجْعَلَهُمْ كَٱلَّذِينَ ءَامَنُوا۟ وَعَمِلُوا۟ ٱلصَّٰلِحَٰتِ سَوَآءً مَّحْيَاهُمْ
وَمَمَاتُهُمْ ۚ سَآءَ مَا يَحْكُمُونَ ﴿٢١﴾ وَخَلَقَ ٱللَّهُ ٱلسَّمَٰوَٰتِ وَٱلْأَرْضَ بِٱلْحَقِّ وَلِتُجْزَىٰ كُلُّ نَفْسٍۭ بِمَا
كَسَبَتْ وَهُمْ لَا يُظْلَمُونَ ﴿٢٢﴾ ﴾

> Do those who do evil deeds think that We shall make them as equal with those who believe and do righteous deeds,—that their life and their death is equal? The judgment that they make is wrong. Allah (God) created the heavens and the earth for just ends,

and in order that each soul may find the recompense of what it has earned, and none of them shall be wronged. (Al-Jathiya [Bowing Down] 45:21–22)

Those who are guided can see their way clearly. Those deprived of guidance are in darkness. The guidance is that of knowledge and faith, which illuminates our way in life so we can understand our objectives and work to achieve them. The darkness is that of ignorance and lack of faith, in which we follow our vain desires and deprive ourselves of God's guidance and mercy.

﴿ أَوَمَن كَانَ مَيْتًا فَأَحْيَيْنَٰهُ وَجَعَلْنَا لَهُۥ نُورًا يَمْشِى بِهِۦ فِى ٱلنَّاسِ كَمَن مَّثَلُهُۥ فِى ٱلظُّلُمَٰتِ
لَيْسَ بِخَارِجٍ مِّنْهَا ۚ كَذَٰلِكَ زُيِّنَ لِلْكَٰفِرِينَ مَا كَانُوا۟ يَعْمَلُونَ ﴾

Can he who was dead, to whom We gave life, and a light whereby he can walk among mankind, be like him who is in the depths of darkness from which he can never come out? Thus to those without faith their own deeds seem pleasing. (Al-An'am [The Cattle] 6:122)

Divine orders are rational and improve our character and behavior. God ordered us to pray not because He needs our prayer but because prayer prevents us from doing shameful and evil deeds. It also reminds us of God and our accountability to Him as we realize that God knows what we do.

﴿ ٱتْلُ مَآ أُوحِىَ إِلَيْكَ مِنَ ٱلْكِتَـٰبِ وَأَقِمِ ٱلصَّلَوٰةَ ۖ إِنَّ ٱلصَّلَوٰةَ تَنْهَىٰ عَنِ ٱلْفَحْشَآءِ
وَٱلْمُنكَرِ ۗ وَلَذِكْرُ ٱللَّهِ أَكْبَرُ ۗ وَٱللَّهُ يَعْلَمُ مَا تَصْنَعُونَ ﴿٤٥﴾ ﴾

> Recite what is sent of the Book to you by inspiration, and establish regular prayer: for prayer restrains from shameful and evil deeds. The remembrance of God is the greatest without doubt, for God knows what you do. (Al-Ankabut [The Spider] 29:45)

Similarly, God ordered us to fast because we learn self-restraint and righteousness from our fast.

﴿ يَـٰٓأَيُّهَا ٱلَّذِينَ ءَامَنُوا۟ كُتِبَ عَلَيْكُمُ ٱلصِّيَامُ كَمَا كُتِبَ عَلَى ٱلَّذِينَ مِن قَبْلِكُمْ لَعَلَّكُمْ تَتَّقُونَ
﴿١٨٣﴾ ﴾

> O you who believe fasting has been ordained on you, as it was ordained on those before you, that you may learn self-restraint and righteousness. (Al-Baqara [The Cow] 2:183)

We are ordered to give in charity because our charity helps the poor and the needy, and we avoid covetousness. God told us that we are rewarded for our charity in many ways, and that the money we gave in charity will be replaced.

﴿ فَٱتَّقُوا ٱللَّهَ مَا ٱسْتَطَعْتُمْ وَٱسْمَعُوا وَأَطِيعُوا وَأَنفِقُوا خَيْرًا لِّأَنفُسِكُمْ ۗ وَمَن يُوقَ شُحَّ نَفْسِهِۦ
فَأُولَٰٓئِكَ هُمُ ٱلْمُفْلِحُونَ ﴿١٦﴾ إِن تُقْرِضُوا ٱللَّهَ قَرْضًا حَسَنًا يُضَٰعِفْهُ لَكُمْ وَيَغْفِرْ لَكُمْ ۚ وَٱللَّهُ شَكُورٌ
حَلِيمٌ ﴿١٧﴾ ﴾

So fear God as much as you can, listen and obey; and spend in charity for the benefit of your own souls. Those saved from the covetousness of their own souls will prosper. If you loan to God a beautiful loan, He will double it to your credit, and He will grant you forgiveness; for God is all-thankful, most-forbearing. (At-Taghabun [Mutual Loss and Gain] 64:16–17)

None of the Qur'anic verses Have Been Proven Wrong

The Qur'an is not a book of science, but none of its verses contradict scientific knowledge. Since the Qur'an is a divine revelation, then the truth of its verses should not contradict proven scientific facts. It is God who gave us our intellect and told us to think, experiment, and look for the truth. Any apparent contradiction between divine scripture and science is due to either wrong understanding of the scripture or an error in our scientific theory. An example is the age of the earth. The Qur'an states that both the heaven and the earth were created in six days. Obviously these are not our days but rather God's days. The Qur'an tells us that one day in the sight of God may be one thousand years or maybe fifty thousand years or may be more.

﴿ وَيَسْتَعْجِلُونَكَ بِٱلْعَذَابِ وَلَن يُخْلِفَ ٱللَّهُ وَعْدَهُۥ ۚ وَإِنَّ يَوْمًا عِندَ رَبِّكَ كَأَلْفِ سَنَةٍ مِّمَّا
تَعُدُّونَ ﴿٤٧﴾ ﴾

> Yet they ask you to hasten on the punishment, but God will not fail in His promise. Indeed a day in the sight of your Lord is like a thousand years of your reckoning. (Al-Hajj [The Pilgrimage] 22:47)

﴿ تَعْرُجُ ٱلْمَلَٰٓئِكَةُ وَٱلرُّوحُ إِلَيْهِ فِى يَوْمٍ كَانَ مِقْدَارُهُۥ خَمْسِينَ أَلْفَ سَنَةٍ ﴿٤﴾ ﴾

> The angels and the spirit ascend unto Him in a day the measure whereof is fifty thousand years. (Al-Ma'rij (Ways of Ascent) 70:4)

There is no contradiction in the Qur'an. Though the Qur'an was revealed interrupted over twenty-three years, there is no contradiction in the Qur'an. Rather, its verses complete and complement one another. The Qur'an asks the question:

﴿ أَفَلَا يَتَدَبَّرُونَ ٱلْقُرْءَانَ ۚ وَلَوْ كَانَ مِنْ عِندِ غَيْرِ ٱللَّهِ لَوَجَدُوا۟ فِيهِ ٱخْتِلَٰفًا كَثِيرًا ﴿٨٢﴾ ﴾

> Do they not ponder on the Qur'an? Had it been from other than God, they would surely have found therein much discrepancy. (An-Nisa' [The Women] 4:82)

Evidence from the Life of Muhammad (PBUH)

Muhammad is God's prophet and messenger. He began to receive God's revelations at age forty and continued to receive the Qur'an till shortly before his death at age sixty-three. Muhammad was illiterate; he could not read nor write. The Qur'an states,

﴿ وَمَا كُنتَ تَتْلُوا۟ مِن قَبْلِهِۦ مِن كِتَٰبٍ وَلَا تَخُطُّهُۥ بِيَمِينِكَ ۖ إِذًا لَّٱرْتَابَ ٱلْمُبْطِلُونَ ﴿٤٨﴾ ﴾

> You were no able, before this revelation, to recite a book or write with your right hand; in that case the talkers of vanity would have doubted. (Al-Ankabut [The Spider] 29:48)

The Qur'an contains information about previous civilizations, the stories of God's prophets and their struggle, and morals and ethics and injunctions. A group of scholars could not produce such a book, let alone a single illiterate person.

No one could produce such a Qur'an. If the Qur'an were the work of a human being, then other humans could produce the likes of such a book. Though many have tried, no one through the centuries has been able to produce the likes of this Qur'an. The challenge still exists today. The Qur'an states,

﴿ قُل لَّئِنِ ٱجْتَمَعَتِ ٱلْإِنسُ وَٱلْجِنُّ عَلَىٰٓ أَن يَأْتُوا۟ بِمِثْلِ هَـٰذَا ٱلْقُرْءَانِ لَا يَأْتُونَ بِمِثْلِهِۦ وَلَوْ
كَانَ بَعْضُهُمْ لِبَعْضٍ ظَهِيرًا ﴿٨٨﴾ ﴾

> Say: "If the whole of mankind and Jinns were to gather together to produce the like of this Qur'an, they could not produce the like thereof, even if they backed up each other with help and support. (Al-Isra' [Night Journey] 17:88)

Are there different versions of the Qur'an like there are different versions of the Bible? When we talk about the Qur'an, we are referring to the Arabic Qur'an. There is only one version of the Arabic Qur'an. It is the same whether we are in the Middle East or in Europe or in America. It is the same Arabic Qur'an that was revealed to Prophet Muhammad (PBUH) and preserved.

How Do Muslims Look at the Qur'an?

Muslims consider the Qur'an the words of God. The Qur'an contains orders that govern the life of Muslims. It is their constitution and main source of knowledge. The tradition (Sunnah) of Prophet Muhammad (PBUH) explains the Qur'an and gives further details how to apply its guidelines and principles in our life.

The Arabic Qur'an is recited every day by Muslims all over the world in their prayers. The Qur'an is a mercy, a guidance, and a cure for the ills in our hearts and a reminder of our accountability to God. It provides a light that illuminates our way in life and lets us understand our duty in serving God.

﴿ يَٰٓأَيُّهَا ٱلنَّاسُ قَدْ جَآءَتْكُم مَّوْعِظَةٌ مِّن رَّبِّكُمْ وَشِفَآءٌ لِّمَا فِى ٱلصُّدُورِ وَهُدًى وَرَحْمَةٌ لِّلْمُؤْمِنِينَ ﴿٥٧﴾ ﴾

O mankind there has come to you an admonition from your Lord, and a healing for the diseases in your hearts, and for those who believe a guidance and a mercy. (Yunus [Jonah] 10:57)

The Qur'an devotes a major portion to morals, ethics, and nobleness of character. Our faith must be confirmed in the way that we obey God and live our lives as righteous servants of God. The Qur'an is the criterion that distinguishes between right and wrong. By its standard are other books judged.

﴿ تَبَارَكَ ٱلَّذِى نَزَّلَ ٱلْفُرْقَانَ عَلَىٰ عَبْدِهِۦ لِيَكُونَ لِلْعَٰلَمِينَ نَذِيرًا ﴿١﴾ ﴾

Blessed is He who sent down the Criterion to His servant, that it may be an admonition to all creatures. (Al-Furqan [The Criterion] 25:1)

Therefore, Muslims use the Qur'an as a standard to judge other revelations. They accept what agrees with the Qur'an but reject what is contrary to Qur'anic teachings, like the divinity of Jesus Christ (PBUH) or the immoral behavior of some prophets mentioned in the Bible.

2

The Message of the Qur'an

We can summarize the teachings of the Qur'an into the following "concepts":

1. Understanding God and our accountability to Him
2. God's divine books
3. God's prophets and messengers
4. Rituals of worship
5. Nobleness of character, morals, and ethics
6. The relationship between human beings
7. Family values

Understanding God and Our Accountability to Him

One of the essential teachings of the Qur'an is the concept of God and our accountability to Him. There is only *one* God who created us and provides for us, and He guides us to His way. He is forgiving and merciful. He knows what we do, and He has full control. We are accountable to Him.

God created mankind to worship Him and to serve Him. Worship is not only prayers or fasting but everything that we do every day in our life, if our motivation is good and if what we do is good and useful. When we help the poor and reach out to those who need our help, then we are worshipping God. When we are honest and do our work to the best of our ability, then we are worshipping God. When we are kind, forgiving, caring, and merciful, then we are worshipping God. The Qur'an summarizes this concept when it states that the goal of worshipping God is to attain *taqwa* (piety, righteousness, goodness, being God-conscious).

﴿ يَٰٓأَيُّهَا ٱلنَّاسُ ٱعْبُدُوا۟ رَبَّكُمُ ٱلَّذِى خَلَقَكُمْ وَٱلَّذِينَ مِن قَبْلِكُمْ لَعَلَّكُمْ تَتَّقُونَ ﴿٢١﴾ ﴾

> O mankind worship your Guardian Lord, who created you and those before you, that you may attain righteousness. (Al-Baqara [The Cow] 2:21)

God's blessings over us as human beings cannot be enumerated. He created us and gave us our faculties and provides for us. He guides us to His way, and He forgives our sins and helps us:

﴿ وَٱللَّهُ أَخْرَجَكُم مِّنۢ بُطُونِ أُمَّهَٰتِكُمْ لَا تَعْلَمُونَ شَيْـًٔا وَجَعَلَ لَكُمُ ٱلسَّمْعَ وَٱلْأَبْصَٰرَ وَٱلْأَفْـِٔدَةَ ۙ لَعَلَّكُمْ تَشْكُرُونَ ﴿٧٨﴾ ﴾

> It is God who brought you forth from the wombs of your mothers when you knew nothing; and *He gave you hearing and sight and intelligence and affections* [emphasis mine], that you may give thanks. (An-Nahl [The Bees] 16:78)

God helps us when we are in trouble.

﴿ أَمَّن يُجِيبُ ٱلْمُضْطَرَّ إِذَا دَعَاهُ وَيَكْشِفُ ٱلسُّوٓءَ وَيَجْعَلُكُمْ خُلَفَآءَ ٱلْأَرْضِ ۗ أَءِلَٰهٌ مَّعَ ٱللَّهِ ۚ قَلِيلًا مَّا تَذَكَّرُونَ ﴿٦٢﴾ ﴾

> Who listens to the distressed when he calls on Him, and who relieves his suffering, and makes you (Mankind) inheritors of the earth? Can there be another god besides Allah? Little it is that you heed. (An-Naml [The Ants] 27:62)

God hears our prayers and answers us.

﴿ وَإِذَا سَأَلَكَ عِبَادِي عَنِّي فَإِنِّي قَرِيبٌ ۖ أُجِيبُ دَعْوَةَ الدَّاعِ إِذَا دَعَانِ ۖ فَلْيَسْتَجِيبُوا لِي وَلْيُؤْمِنُوا
بِي لَعَلَّهُمْ يَرْشُدُونَ ﴿١٨٦﴾

> When My servants ask you concerning Me, I am indeed close to them; I respond to the prayer of every supplicant when he calls on Me; Let them also listen to My call, and believe in Me, that they may walk in the right way. (Al-Baqara [The Cow] 2:186)

Despite God's many blessings, man wrongs himself and commits sin, but God is often forgiving, most merciful.

﴿ وَإِن تَعُدُّوا نِعْمَةَ اللَّهِ لَا تُحْصُوهَا ۗ إِنَّ اللَّهَ لَغَفُورٌ رَّحِيمٌ ﴿١٨﴾ ﴾

> If you enumerate the blessings of God, you would not be able to count them up, but God is often-forgiving, most-merciful. (An-Nahl [The Bees] 16:18)

As human beings, we are limited in our ability to understand the nature of God. We cannot see Him, but we see His creation and feel and understand His blessings. We see His power, majesty, and wisdom in the creation around us. The Qur'an explains that there is nothing like God and that the way to understand Him is to understand His creation and witness His blessings. We should not think of Him as a human being because we then impart to Him weakness and fallibility.

﴿ بَدِيعُ ٱلسَّمَٰوَٰتِ وَٱلْأَرْضِ ۖ أَنَّىٰ يَكُونُ لَهُۥ وَلَدٌ وَلَمْ تَكُن لَّهُۥ صَٰحِبَةٌ ۖ وَخَلَقَ كُلَّ شَىْءٍ ۖ وَهُوَ
بِكُلِّ شَىْءٍ عَلِيمٌ ﴿١٠١﴾ ذَٰلِكُمُ ٱللَّهُ رَبُّكُمْ ۖ لَآ إِلَٰهَ إِلَّا هُوَ ۖ خَٰلِقُ كُلِّ شَىْءٍ فَٱعْبُدُوهُ ۚ وَهُوَ عَلَىٰ
كُلِّ شَىْءٍ وَكِيلٌ ﴿١٠٢﴾ لَّا تُدْرِكُهُ ٱلْأَبْصَٰرُ وَهُوَ يُدْرِكُ ٱلْأَبْصَٰرَ ۖ وَهُوَ ٱللَّطِيفُ ٱلْخَبِيرُ ﴿١٠٣﴾ ﴾

Wonderful originator of the heavens and the earth. How can He have a son when He has no wife? He created all things, and He has full knowledge of all things. That is God, your Lord. There is no god but He, the Creator of all things, then worship Him, and He has power to dispose of all affairs. No vision can grasp Him, but His grasp is over all things. He is subtle, well aware. (Al-An'am [The Cattle] 6:101–103)

We live in the present time and know what happened in the past but do not know what will happen in the future. Time is irrelevant to God, for He knows the unseen, and He knows what will occur in the future. His will is over all things, and when He decrees something, He says, "Be," and it becomes.

﴿ إِنَّمَا قَوْلُنَا لِشَىْءٍ إِذَآ أَرَدْنَٰهُ أَن نَّقُولَ لَهُۥ كُن فَيَكُونُ ﴿٤٠﴾ ﴾

To anything which We have willed, We but say: "Be" and it is." (An-Nahl [The Bees] 16:40)

When we call on God and pray to Him, we understand our dependence on Him and that He controls our destiny. Therefore, calling on God is part of faith.

﴿ وَقَالَ رَبُّكُمُ ٱدْعُونِيٓ أَسْتَجِبْ لَكُمْ ۚ إِنَّ ٱلَّذِينَ يَسْتَكْبِرُونَ عَنْ عِبَادَتِي سَيَدْخُلُونَ جَهَنَّمَ دَاخِرِينَ ﴿٦٠﴾ ﴾

> Your Lord said: "Call on Me, I will answer you; but those who are too arrogant to serve Me, will surely enter Hell humiliated." (Ghafir [Forgiving] 40:60)

In addition to God's ability and creation, the Qur'an explains God's names or attributes as another way of knowing and understanding God.

﴿ وَلِلَّهِ ٱلْأَسْمَآءُ ٱلْحُسْنَىٰ فَٱدْعُوهُ بِهَا ﴾

> To God belongs the most beautiful names (attributes of perfection), so call on Him by them. (Al-Araf 7:180)

We will briefly discuss some of God's names or attributes.

God Is Forgiving

﴿ وَإِنِّي لَغَفَّارٌ لِّمَن تَابَ وَءَامَنَ وَعَمِلَ صَٰلِحًا ثُمَّ ٱهْتَدَىٰ ﴿٨٢﴾ ﴾

> But without doubt I am He that forgives again and again, to those who repent, believe and do right, who then are on true guidance. (Ta Ha 20:82)

God's forgiveness is therefore for those who realize their mistakes, turn to Him in repentance, confirm their faith, work righteous deeds, and are willing to receive guidance.

When we turn to God in repentance and seek His forgiveness, He promises to blot our sins and turn our evil into good:

﴿ إِلَّا مَن تَابَ وَءَامَنَ وَعَمِلَ عَمَلًا صَٰلِحًا فَأُوْلَٰٓئِكَ يُبَدِّلُ ٱللَّهُ سَيِّـَٔاتِهِمْ حَسَنَٰتٍ ۗ وَكَانَ ٱللَّهُ غَفُورًا رَّحِيمًا ﴿٧٠﴾ ﴾

> Unless he repents, believes, and work righteous deeds, for God will change the evil of such persons into good, for God is often-forgiving, most-merciful. (Al-Furqan [The Criterion] 25:70)

God Is Merciful

كَتَبَ عَلَىٰ نَفْسِهِ ٱلرَّحْمَةَ

He ordained on Himself the rule of mercy. (Al-An'am [The Cattle] 6:12)

God's special mercy is for those who confirm their faith, who are righteous, and who give in charity:

وَرَحْمَتِي وَسِعَتْ كُلَّ شَيْءٍ ۚ فَسَأَكْتُبُهَا لِلَّذِينَ يَتَّقُونَ وَيُؤْتُونَ ٱلزَّكَوٰةَ وَٱلَّذِينَ هُم بِـَٔايَـٰتِنَا يُؤْمِنُونَ ﴿١٥٦﴾

But My mercy extends to all things. (That mercy) I shall ordain to those who do right, and give in charity and those who believe in Our [Our is not pleural but majestic for God] signs. (Al-Araf 7:156)

God Is Just

No soul is wronged. God's justice is perfect. We are rewarded according to the best of our deeds.

﴿ إِنَّ ٱللَّهَ لَا يَظْلِمُ ٱلنَّاسَ شَيْـًٔا وَلَـٰكِنَّ ٱلنَّاسَ أَنفُسَهُمْ يَظْلِمُونَ ﴿٤٤﴾ ﴾

Indeed God will not wrong man in the least, it is man that wrongs his own soul. (Yunus [Jonah] 10:44)

The scales of justice are perfect on the Day of Judgment, and everything is taken into account.

﴿ وَنَضَعُ ٱلْمَوَٰزِينَ ٱلْقِسْطَ لِيَوْمِ ٱلْقِيَـٰمَةِ فَلَا تُظْلَمُ نَفْسٌ شَيْـًٔا ۖ وَإِن كَانَ مِثْقَالَ حَبَّةٍ مِّنْ
خَرْدَلٍ أَتَيْنَا بِهَا ۗ وَكَفَىٰ بِنَا حَـٰسِبِينَ ﴿٤٧﴾ ﴾

> We shall set up scales of justice for the Day of Judgment, so that no soul is wronged in the least; If there be no more than the weight of a mustard seed, We will bring it to account; enough are We to take account. (Al-Anbiya [The Prophets] 21:47)

God Knows What We Do

We cannot hide anything from Him. Whether we conceal or reveal what we say or do, God is well aware of all things.

﴿ قُلْ إِن تُخْفُوا۟ مَا فِى صُدُورِكُمْ أَوْ تُبْدُوهُ يَعْلَمْهُ ٱللَّهُ ۗ وَيَعْلَمُ مَا فِى ٱلسَّمَـٰوَٰتِ وَمَا فِى ٱلْأَرْضِ

> Say: "Whether you hide what is in your hearts or reveal it, God knows it all; He knows what is in the heavens and what is on earth. And God has power over all things." (Al-Imran [The Family of Imran] 3:29)

God Provides for His Servants

Not a living thing on earth for whom God does not provide sustenance.

﴿ وَكَأَيِّن مِّن دَآبَّةٍ لَّا تَحْمِلُ رِزْقَهَا ٱللَّهُ يَرْزُقُهَا وَإِيَّاكُمْ ۚ وَهُوَ ٱلسَّمِيعُ ٱلْعَلِ

> How many are the creatures that carry not their own sustenance? It is God who feeds them and you, for He hears and knows all things. (Al-Ankabut [The Spider] 29:60)

Whatever we give in charity to help others, God will replace.

﴿ قُلْ إِنَّ رَبِّى يَبْسُطُ ٱلرِّزْقَ لِمَن يَشَآءُ مِنْ عِبَادِهِۦ وَيَقْدِرُ لَهُۥ ۚ وَمَآ أَنفَقْتُم مِّن شَىْءٍ فَهُوَ يُخْلِفُهُۥ ۖ
وَهُوَ خَيْرُ ٱلرَّٰزِقِينَ ﴿٣٩﴾ ﴾

> Say: "My Lord enlarges and restricts the sustenance to such of His servants as He pleases; Nothing that you spend in the least in His cause but He replaces it, for He is the best of those who grant sustenance." (Sa'Ba 34:39)

Accountability and the Day of Judgment

After we die we will be resurrected to stand judgment. We have to account for everything that we have done in our lives. Prophet Muhammad (PBUH) stated that every human being will be asked to account for four areas (narrated by Tirmidhi): his whole life (what has he done?), his youth (did he waste his energy and abuse it or do right?), his money (how did he earn it? how did he spend it?), and his knowledge and wisdom (what did he do with it?).

The Qur'an warns us of the day when each soul will plead for itself and is held accountable:

﴿ وَٱتَّقُواْ يَوْمًا تُرْجَعُونَ فِيهِ إِلَى ٱللَّهِ ۖ ثُمَّ تُوَفَّىٰ كُلُّ نَفْسٍ مَّا كَسَبَتْ وَهُمْ لَا يُظْلَمُونَ ۝ ﴾

> And fear the day when you shall be brought back to God, then shall every soul be paid what it earned, and none shall be dealt with unjustly. (Al-Baqara [The Cow] 2:281)

The Qur'an also explains that we will be rewarded or punished on the Day of Judgment and that true success is to avoid hellfire and enter paradise.

﴿ كُلُّ نَفْسٍ ذَآئِقَةُ ٱلْمَوْتِ ۗ وَإِنَّمَا تُوَفَّوْنَ أُجُورَكُمْ يَوْمَ ٱلْقِيَٰمَةِ ۖ فَمَن زُحْزِحَ عَنِ ٱلنَّارِ
وَأُدْخِلَ ٱلْجَنَّةَ فَقَدْ فَازَ ۗ وَمَا ٱلْحَيَوٰةُ ٱلدُّنْيَآ إِلَّا مَتَٰعُ ٱلْغُرُورِ ۝ ﴾

> Every soul shall have a taste of death; only on the Day of Judgment shall you be paid your full recompense. Only he who is saved from the Fire and admitted to the Garden will have succeeded; for the life of this world is but goods and chattels of deception. (Al-Imran [The Family of Imran] 3:185)

Those who are righteous will be rewarded according to the best of their deeds.

﴿ مَنْ عَمِلَ صَٰلِحًا مِّن ذَكَرٍ أَوْ أُنثَىٰ وَهُوَ مُؤْمِنٌ فَلَنُحْيِيَنَّهُۥ حَيَوٰةً طَيِّبَةً ۖ وَلَنَجْزِيَنَّهُمْ أَجْرَهُم بِأَحْسَنِ مَا كَانُوا۟ يَعْمَلُونَ ﴿٩٧﴾ ﴾

> Whoever works righteousness, man or woman, and has faith, indeed to him We will give a life that is good and pure, and We will bestow on such their reward according to the best of their actions. (An-Nahl [The Bees] 16:97)

A bad deed is dealt with as only one bad deed, but a good deed is rewarded ten times or more.

﴿ مَن جَآءَ بِٱلْحَسَنَةِ فَلَهُۥ عَشْرُ أَمْثَالِهَا ۖ وَمَن جَآءَ بِٱلسَّيِّئَةِ فَلَا يُجْزَىٰٓ إِلَّا مِثْلَهَا وَهُمْ لَا يُظْلَمُونَ ﴿١٦٠﴾ ﴾

> He that does good deeds shall have ten times as much to his credit, he that does evil shall only be

recompensed according to his evil. No wrong shall be done unto them. (Al-An'am [The Cattle] 6:160)

Those who confirmed their faith and patiently persevered will be rewarded with paradise, to live there forever:

﴿ وَالَّذِينَ آمَنُوا وَعَمِلُوا الصَّالِحَاتِ لَنُبَوِّئَنَّهُم مِّنَ الْجَنَّةِ غُرَفًا تَجْرِي مِن تَحْتِهَا الْأَنْهَارُ خَالِدِينَ
فِيهَا ۚ نِعْمَ أَجْرُ الْعَامِلِينَ ﴿٥٨﴾ الَّذِينَ صَبَرُوا وَعَلَىٰ رَبِّهِمْ يَتَوَكَّلُونَ ﴿٥٩﴾ ﴾

> Those who believe and work deeds of righteousness, to them shall We give a home in heaven, lofty mansions beneath which rivers flow, to dwell therein forever; an excellent reward for those who do right. Those who persevere in patience, and put their trust in their Lord. (Al-Ankabut [The Spider] 29:58–59)

In contrast, those who disobeyed God and followed their vain desires will be punished in hellfire. They disregarded the signs of God and only cared for the material things in life.

﴿ إِنَّ الَّذِينَ لَا يَرْجُونَ لِقَاءَنَا وَرَضُوا بِالْحَيَاةِ الدُّنْيَا وَاطْمَأَنُّوا بِهَا وَالَّذِينَ هُمْ عَنْ
آيَاتِنَا غَافِلُونَ ﴿٧﴾ أُولَٰئِكَ مَأْوَاهُمُ النَّارُ بِمَا كَانُوا يَكْسِبُونَ ﴿٨﴾ ﴾

> Those who rest not their hopes on their meeting with us, but are pleased and satisfied with the life of the present, and those who heed not Our signs, their abode is the Fire, because of the evil they earned. (Yunus [Jonah] 10:7–8)

They will be suffering and pleading in the fire, but no one can/will help them, for they disregarded the warning.

﴿ وَالَّذِينَ كَفَرُوا لَهُمْ نَارُ جَهَنَّمَ لَا يُقْضَىٰ عَلَيْهِمْ فَيَمُوتُوا وَلَا يُخَفَّفُ عَنْهُم مِّنْ عَذَابِهَا ۚ كَذَٰلِكَ
نَجْزِي كُلَّ كَفُورٍ ﴿٣٦﴾ وَهُمْ يَصْطَرِخُونَ فِيهَا رَبَّنَا أَخْرِجْنَا نَعْمَلْ صَالِحًا غَيْرَ الَّذِي كُنَّا
نَعْمَلُ ۚ أَوَلَمْ نُعَمِّرْكُم مَّا يَتَذَكَّرُ فِيهِ مَن تَذَكَّرَ وَجَاءَكُمُ النَّذِيرُ ۖ فَذُوقُوا فَمَا لِلظَّالِمِينَ مِن نَّصِيرٍ
﴿٣٧﴾ ﴾

> But those who reject faith, for them will be the Fire of Hell; no term shall be determined for them so they should die, nor their suffering shall be lightened for them. Thus do We reward every ungrateful one! Therein they will cry aloud: "Our Lord bring us out we shall work righteousness, not the deeds we used to do". Did We not give long enough life so that he that would should receive admonition? And the Warner came to you, so taste! For the wrong-doer there is no helper. (Fatir [Originator] 35:36–37)

As long as we avoid the major sins, our minor sins will be forgiven. The major sins are the following:

1. Worshipping someone else besides God
2. Being unkind to our parents or treating them wrongly
3. Killing a soul that God has made sacred

4. Committing adultery
5. Drinking alcohol and gambling
6. Lying
7. Cheating or giving false measure or weight
8. Being unkind or abusive to orphans
9. Not keeping our promises or being untrue to our covenants
10. Following a path other than the straight path of God

We must prove our faith in this life before we die. After we die regrets will not help, and there is no second chance. The Qur'an states,

وَأَنفِقُوا۟ مِن مَّا رَزَقْنَـٰكُم مِّن قَبْلِ أَن يَأْتِىَ أَحَدَكُمُ ٱلْمَوْتُ فَيَقُولَ رَبِّ لَوْلَآ أَخَّرْتَنِىٓ إِلَىٰٓ أَجَلٍ
قَرِيبٍ فَأَصَّدَّقَ وَأَكُن مِّنَ ٱلصَّـٰلِحِينَ ﴿١٠﴾ وَلَن يُؤَخِّرَ ٱللَّهُ نَفْسًا إِذَا جَآءَ أَجَلُهَا ۚ وَٱللَّهُ خَبِيرٌۢ بِمَا
تَعْمَلُونَ ﴿١١﴾

> And spend out of what We provided for you, before death comes to one of you and he should say: "My Lord why did You not give me respite for a little while? I should then have given in charity and should have done good deeds." But God will not give respite to no soul when its appointed time has come, and God is well-acquainted with all that you do. (Al-Munafiqun [The Hypocrites] 63:10–11)

The Concept of Intercession

No angel or prophet or righteous person can intercede without God giving them the right or power to intercede. On the Day of Judgment God will allow Prophet Muhammad (PBUH) to intercede on behalf of those who confirmed their faith. Intercession is only allowed on behalf of those whom God has accepted. The Qur'an confirms these concepts:

﴿ ۞ وَكَم مِّن مَّلَكٍ فِي ٱلسَّمَٰوَٰتِ لَا تُغۡنِي شَفَٰعَتُهُمۡ شَيۡـًٔا إِلَّا مِنۢ بَعۡدِ أَن يَأۡذَنَ ٱللَّهُ لِمَن يَشَآءُ وَيَرۡضَىٰٓ ﴿٢٦﴾ ﴾

> How many angels are in heaven, their intercession will not avail nothing except after God has given permission for whom He pleases, and that is acceptable to Him. (An-Najm [The Star] 53:26)

﴿ وَلَا تَنفَعُ ٱلشَّفَٰعَةُ عِندَهُۥٓ إِلَّا لِمَنۡ أَذِنَ لَهُۥ ﴾

> No intercession can avail with Him, except for those for whom God has granted permission. (Saba 34:23)

God's Divine Books and God's Prophets and Messengers

The Qur'an came to confirm previous divine revelations, namely the Torah of Moses and the Gospel of Jesus.

﴿ نَزَّلَ عَلَيْكَ ٱلْكِتَٰبَ بِٱلْحَقِّ مُصَدِّقًا لِّمَا بَيْنَ يَدَيْهِ وَأَنزَلَ ٱلتَّوْرَىٰةَ وَٱلْإِنجِيلَ ۝ مِن قَبْلُ
هُدًى لِّلنَّاسِ وَأَنزَلَ ٱلْفُرْقَانَ ۗ

> He (God) sent down the Book to you in truth, confirming what came before it, and He sent down the Torah and Gospel, before as a guidance to mankind, and He sent down the Criterion. (Al-Imran [The Family of Imran] 3:3–4)

Muslims believe in previous divine revelations as they believe in all the prophets and messengers sent by God before Muhammad (PBUH).

﴿ قُولُوٓا۟ ءَامَنَّا بِٱللَّهِ وَمَآ أُنزِلَ إِلَيْنَا وَمَآ أُنزِلَ إِلَىٰٓ إِبْرَٰهِـۧمَ وَإِسْمَٰعِيلَ وَإِسْحَٰقَ وَيَعْقُوبَ وَٱلْأَسْبَاطِ
وَمَآ أُوتِىَ مُوسَىٰ وَعِيسَىٰ وَمَآ أُوتِىَ ٱلنَّبِيُّونَ مِن رَّبِّهِمْ لَا نُفَرِّقُ بَيْنَ أَحَدٍ مِّنْهُمْ وَنَحْنُ لَهُۥ مُسْلِمُونَ
۝ ﴾

> Say: "We believe in God, and what was sent down to us, and what was sent down to Abraham, Ismail, Isaac, Jacob and the tribes, and what the prophets got from their Lord; we do not distinguish between

any of them, and we submit to God in Islam." (Al-Baqara [The Cow] 2:136)

Muslims believe in Abraham, Moses, and Jesus as messengers sent from God to their own people. Muhammad came to complete the divine message and to confirm the work of previous messengers.

﴿ ۞ شَرَعَ لَكُم مِّنَ ٱلدِّينِ مَا وَصَّىٰ بِهِۦ نُوحًا وَٱلَّذِىٓ أَوْحَيْنَآ إِلَيْكَ وَمَا وَصَّيْنَا بِهِۦٓ إِبْرَٰهِيمَ وَمُوسَىٰ
وَعِيسَىٰٓ ۖ أَنْ أَقِيمُوا۟ ٱلدِّينَ وَلَا تَتَفَرَّقُوا۟ فِيهِ ۚ كَبُرَ عَلَى ٱلْمُشْرِكِينَ مَا تَدْعُوهُمْ إِلَيْهِ ۚ ٱللَّهُ يَجْتَبِىٓ إِلَيْهِ
مَن يَشَآءُ وَيَهْدِىٓ إِلَيْهِ مَن يُنِيبُ ﴿١٣﴾ ﴾

God established for you the religion, the same as He enjoined on Noah, that which We have sent by inspiration to you, and that which We enjoined on Abraham, Moses and Jesus, namely that you should remain steadfast in religion and make no divisions therein. (Ash-Shuraa [Consultation] 42:13)

Therefore, in Islam the message of all God's prophets and messengers came from the same source, the one and only God. The message is similar, namely to remind people of their duty to serve God and their accountability to Him. The Qur'an explains that to God there is only one religion: Islam or submission to His will. All of God's prophets submitted to God; therefore, they were Muslims.

﴿إِنَّ ٱلدِّينَ عِندَ ٱللَّهِ ٱلْإِسْلَٰمُ﴾

> Religion to God is Islam (submitting to His will). (Al-Imran [The Family of Imran] 3:19)

All of God's prophets and messengers were therefore Muslims, in the sense that they submitted to God. For example, Abraham and Jacob (Israel) are noted in the Qur'an as advising their children not to die except as Muslims.

﴿وَوَصَّىٰ بِهَآ إِبْرَٰهِـۧمُ بَنِيهِ وَيَعْقُوبُ يَٰبَنِيَّ إِنَّ ٱللَّهَ ٱصْطَفَىٰ لَكُمُ ٱلدِّينَ فَلَا تَمُوتُنَّ إِلَّا وَأَنتُم
مُّسْلِمُونَ ﴿١٣٢﴾﴾

> The advice that Abraham and Jacob gave to their children was: "My children God has chosen for you the religion, therefore die not except as Muslims (submitting to God)." (Al-Baqara [The Cow] 2:132)

The Qur'an praises Prophet Abraham as a devout servant of God and as one of the righteous. It orders Muslims to follow the way of Abraham.

﴿إِنَّ إِبْرَٰهِيمَ كَانَ أُمَّةً قَانِتًا لِّلَّهِ حَنِيفًا وَلَمْ يَكُ مِنَ ٱلْمُشْرِكِينَ ﴿١٢٠﴾ شَاكِرًا لِّأَنْعُمِهِ ۚ ٱجْتَبَىٰهُ
وَهَدَىٰهُ إِلَىٰ صِرَٰطٍ مُّسْتَقِيمٍ ﴿١٢١﴾ وَءَاتَيْنَٰهُ فِى ٱلدُّنْيَا حَسَنَةً ۖ وَإِنَّهُۥ فِى ٱلْءَاخِرَةِ لَمِنَ ٱلصَّٰلِحِينَ ﴿١٢٢﴾
ثُمَّ أَوْحَيْنَآ إِلَيْكَ أَنِ ٱتَّبِعْ مِلَّةَ إِبْرَٰهِيمَ حَنِيفًا ۖ وَمَا كَانَ مِنَ ٱلْمُشْرِكِينَ ﴿١٢٣﴾﴾

> Indeed Abraham was devout, an example to follow, and he worshipped none but God. He was grateful for God's blessings; God chose him and guided him to a straight path. We gave him good in this life, and in the Hereafter he is among the righteous. Then we inspired to you (O Muhammad) that you should follow the way of Abraham, for he was devout and worshipped none but God. (An-Nahl [The Bees] 16:120–123)

God's prophets explained God's message, and applied the message on themselves. Therefore, they became examples to follow in their character and behavior. The Qur'an tells us to follow the example of Prophet Muhammad (PBUH)

﴿ لَّقَدْ كَانَ لَكُمْ فِي رَسُولِ ٱللَّهِ أُسْوَةٌ حَسَنَةٌ

> You have in the messenger of God a good example to follow. (Al-Ahzab [The Confederates] 33:21)

So How Do Muslims Deal with the Bible?

Whatever agrees with the Qur'an is accepted, like the duty of mankind to worship God and that as human beings we are accountable to God. Morals and ethics in the Bible are well accepted, but concepts that contradict the teachings of the Qur'an are not accepted, like the Trinity or the divinity of Jesus Christ (PBUH). Also the immoral behavior of some of God's prophets mentioned in the Old Testament cannot be accepted by Muslims because God's prophets possess noble character and will not commit a major sin like lying, cheating, killing, or adultery.

The Qur'an controls previous divine revelations and corrects any mistakes humans introduced into the scripture. The Qur'an states,

﴿ وَأَنزَلْنَآ إِلَيْكَ ٱلْكِتَٰبَ بِٱلْحَقِّ مُصَدِّقًا لِّمَا بَيْنَ يَدَيْهِ مِنَ ٱلْكِتَٰبِ وَمُهَيْمِنًا عَلَيْهِ ۖ فَٱحْكُم
بَيْنَهُم بِمَآ أَنزَلَ ٱللَّهُ ۖ وَلَا تَتَّبِعْ أَهْوَآءَهُمْ عَمَّا جَآءَكَ مِنَ ٱلْحَقِّ ۚ

> To you We sent the scripture in truth, confirming the scripture that came before it, and guarding it in safety; So judge between them by what Allah has revealed, and follow not their vain desires, diverging from the truth that has come to you. (Al-Maidah [The Table] 5:48)

Rituals of Worship

Muslims are ordered in the Qur'an to pray, to give charity, and to fast the month of Ramadan. Those who can afford the journey are told to perform hajj (pilgrimage) to Mecca. These are the rituals of worship.

Prayer

Prayer is done in a structured way, following what Prophet Muhammad (PBUH) told us to do. Muslims pray five times every day:

1. Dawn prayer before the sun rises
2. Noon prayer
3. Afternoon prayer
4. Prayer at sunset
5. Night prayer

These are the five obligatory prayers done every day in the life of a Muslim. In addition, Muslims offer optional prayers, following the tradition of Prophet Muhammad (PBUH). These prayers follow a certain structure, which consists of three phases:

1. Standing up, reciting the Qur'an in Arabic
2. Bowing down, celebrating God
3. Prostrating, celebrating God

When these three phases are completed, then one rakat is done. The dawn prayer is two rakats; the noon prayer, four; the afternoon prayer, four; the sunset prayer, three; and the night prayer, four. Therefore, the Muslim prays seventeen rakats each day of his life. Only the Arabic Qur'an is accepted in prayer.

Prayer brings us closer to God as we recite His own words and stand up praying to Him, seeking His forgiveness, guidance, and mercy. The Qur'an orders Muslims to pray and explains the benefit of prayer:

﴿ أَقِمِ ٱلصَّلَوٰةَ لِدُلُوكِ ٱلشَّمْسِ إِلَىٰ غَسَقِ ٱلَّيْلِ وَقُرْءَانَ ٱلْفَجْرِ ۖ إِنَّ قُرْءَانَ ٱلْفَجْرِ كَانَ مَشْهُودًا
﴿٧٨﴾ ﴾

> Establish regular prayers at the sun's decline till the darkness of the night, and the recital of the Qur'an at Dawn prayer, for the recital at Dawn is witnessed. (Al-Isra' [Night Journey] 17:78)

﴿ ٱتْلُ مَآ أُوحِىَ إِلَيْكَ مِنَ ٱلْكِتَٰبِ وَأَقِمِ ٱلصَّلَوٰةَ ۖ إِنَّ ٱلصَّلَوٰةَ تَنْهَىٰ عَنِ ٱلْفَحْشَآءِ
وَٱلْمُنكَرِ ۗ وَلَذِكْرُ ٱللَّهِ أَكْبَرُ ۗ وَٱللَّهُ يَعْلَمُ مَا تَصْنَعُونَ ﴿٤٥﴾ ﴾

> Recite what is sent to you of the Book by inspiration, and establish regular prayer; for prayer restrains from shameful and evil deeds; and remembrance of Allah is the greatest without doubt; and Allah knows the deeds that you do. (Al-Ankabut [The Spider] 29:45)

There are many benefits of prayer, and our prayer to God has great rewards. Prayer restrains us from doing shameful and evil deeds. Prayer brings us closer to God and reminds us of our accountability to Him. We recite the Qur'an during our prayers, and the Qur'an is a guidance and a mercy. We learn discipline and placing our priorities properly. We learn obedience, devotion, and humility. Prayer in congregation allows Muslims to know one another.

The congregational prayers occur every week at noontime on Friday. It is called the Jumu'a or Friday prayer. Also, in the month of Ramadan, Muslims fast and perform their prayers in congregation at the mosque at night prayer, followed by additional optional prayers. During the two eids (festivals), Muslims start their celebration by prayer.

Charity

Charity is also obligatory for Muslims who are able to give. Muslims are obligated to give 2.5 percent of their income to the poor, the needy, and other entities who need their charitable gifts. This charity is called zakat; meaning, it purifies our money and liberates our souls from greed. The wealth of the community is circulated to achieve social justice and create jobs and improve the economy. Those who hoard their money and do not give in to charity are threatened with severe punishment. The Qur'an confirms these concepts. The reward for charity is that our good deeds are multiplied to our credit, our sins are forgiven, and God appreciates our effort.

﴿ إِن تُقْرِضُوا اللَّهَ قَرْضًا حَسَنًا يُضَاعِفْهُ لَكُمْ وَيَغْفِرْ لَكُمْ ۚ وَاللَّهُ شَكُورٌ حَلِيمٌ ﴿١٧﴾ ﴾

> If you loan to God a beautiful loan, He will double it to your credit, and He will grant you forgiveness, for God is all-thankful, most-forbearing. (At-Taghabun [Mutual Loss and Gain] 64:17)

The goal of charity is to help the poor and the needy, but it should be done in a way that does not harm their feelings or dignity. The Qur'an warns Muslims against improper behavior.

﴿ قَوْلٌ مَّعْرُوفٌ وَمَغْفِرَةٌ خَيْرٌ مِّن صَدَقَةٍ يَتْبَعُهَا أَذًى ۗ وَاللَّهُ غَنِيٌّ حَلِيمٌ ﴿٢٦٣﴾ يَا أَيُّهَا الَّذِينَ آمَنُوا
لَا تُبْطِلُوا صَدَقَاتِكُم بِالْمَنِّ وَالْأَذَىٰ

> Kind words and covering of faults are better than charity followed by injury. God is free of all wants, and He is most-forbearing. O you who believe cancel not your charity by reminders of your generosity or by injury. (Al-Baqara [The Cow] 2:263–264)

Fasting Ramadan

Fasting is an obligation for Muslims during the month of Ramadan, which is the ninth month of the lunar year. During this blessed month, Muslims fast from dawn till sunset and abstain from food, drink, and desires. They eat and drink after sunset. This fast lasts for a whole month.

The object of the fast is to learn patience, self-restraint, and commitment and to obey God and get close to Him. During the fast we learn proper manners as a fasting person is not allowed to use bad language, get angry, engage in fights, lie, cheat, or harm other people. Such a wrong behavior is not proper for a person who is fasting to please God. Prophet Muhammad (PBUH) told us that if we lie or cheat or give false witness, then there is no need for us to stop eating or drinking because we have cancelled our fast. Fasting has great rewards as the prophet (PBUH) explained, and that reward is forgiveness of sin and the good pleasure of God and His paradise. The Qur'an explains that the goal of fasting is to achieve *taqwa* (piety and righteousness).

﴿ يَٰٓأَيُّهَا ٱلَّذِينَ ءَامَنُواْ كُتِبَ عَلَيۡكُمُ ٱلصِّيَامُ كَمَا كُتِبَ عَلَى ٱلَّذِينَ مِن قَبۡلِكُمۡ لَعَلَّكُمۡ تَتَّقُونَ ١٨٣ ﴾

> O you who believe fasting has been ordained on you, as it was ordained on those before you, that you may achieve Taqwa (self-restraint and righteousness). (Al-Baqara [The Cow] 2:183)

Hajj (Pilgrimage)

Hajj or pilgrimage is visiting the holy places in and around Macca. During this journey a pilgrim circles the Kaaba as a form of prayer, remembering prophets Ibrahim and Isma'il, who built this house of worship to God. Then the pilgrim walks between Safa and Marwah. These are two hills next to the Kaaba. During this walk the pilgrim pays homage to Hajir, the wife of Prophet Ibrahim and the mother of Prophet Ishmael, who was left in the desert with her infant son. Then the pilgrim stands in the valley of Arafat, praying to God and seeking His forgiveness and His guidance. The pilgrim makes a covenant with God that he will obey God and live his life as God has commanded.

Therefore, hajj is a new beginning and should be done early rather than late. A pilgrim in Arafat remembers the Day of Judgment, when everyone will be waiting as God judges His servants and each soul is held accountable. Then the pilgrim goes to Mina to perform certain rituals, like offering a sacrifice and stoning the devil. Hajj is a journey of purification as we leave our preoccupation with this world and journey to God, making a pledge to obey Him and to seek His pleasure and forgiveness.

Morals and Ethics in the Qur'an

A great deal of the Qur'an deals with morals and ethics and noble character. Prophet Muhammad (PBUH) explained that the goal of his mission is to implement the noblest character (narrated by Bayhaqi). He told us,

> Be conscious of God at all times, and follow a bad deed with a good deed, it will wipe it out, and live and interact with others on the basis of morals and noble character. (Narrated by Abu Dawood)

Such noble character includes the following:

1. Being truthful in word and deed
2. Being righteous
3. Being patient and persevering
4. Being just and not wronging others
5. Being kind, forgiving, and merciful
6. Being humble and not arrogant
7. Being devoted and sincere in serving God
8. Seeking knowledge, proper understanding, and wisdom
9. Loving others, caring for their welfare, and reaching out to help those who need our help
10. Thanking God and acknowledging His blessings
11. Doing our work to the best of our ability and being honest
12. Never giving up hope of God's mercy during difficult times and working through our difficulty

13. Seeking God's forgiveness for our sins and doing good to wipe our evil and shameful deeds
14. Not harboring ill feelings toward others or feeling jealous or envious; rather, praying to God to guide them

We will discuss some of these attributes and concepts when we talk about the similarities between the Qur'an and the Bible.

Family Values

The Qur'an explains that the intimate relationship between the spouses is based on kindness, love, and mercy and that such a relationship affords peace and happiness for each of the spouses. Such a relationship is a blessing from God and described as one of the signs of God in order that we may cherish our spouses and acknowledge God's blessing.

﴿ وَمِنْ ءَايَـٰتِهِۦٓ أَنْ خَلَقَ لَكُم مِّنْ أَنفُسِكُمْ أَزْوَٰجًا لِّتَسْكُنُوٓا۟ إِلَيْهَا وَجَعَلَ بَيْنَكُم مَّوَدَّةً وَرَحْمَةً
إِنَّ فِى ذَٰلِكَ لَءَايَـٰتٍ لِّقَوْمٍ يَتَفَكَّرُونَ ﴿٢١﴾ ﴾

> And among His signs is that He created for you spouses from among yourselves, in order that you may find peace and happiness in them; and He established your relationship on the basis of kindness, love and mercy. Indeed in this are signs for those who reflect. (Ar-Rum [The Romans] 30:21)

The Qur'an tells us to treat our wives well and to take care of them.

ﵟوَعَاشِرُوهُنَّ بِٱلۡمَعۡرُوفِۚﵞ

> And live with them on equitable terms. (An-Nisa' [The Women] 4:19)

Prophet Muhammad (PBUH) explained further that the greatest are those who are best to their wives and families. He said, "The best amongst you, are those who are best to their wives and families" (narrated by Bukhari).

The Qur'an stresses our obligation to be kind to our parents and to respect them and take care of them, especially in their old age.

﴿ ۞ وَقَضَىٰ رَبُّكَ أَلَّا تَعۡبُدُوٓاْ إِلَّآ إِيَّاهُ وَبِٱلۡوَٰلِدَيۡنِ إِحۡسَٰنًاۚ إِمَّا يَبۡلُغَنَّ عِندَكَ ٱلۡكِبَرَ أَحَدُهُمَآ أَوۡ
كِلَاهُمَا فَلَا تَقُل لَّهُمَآ أُفّٖ وَلَا تَنۡهَرۡهُمَا وَقُل لَّهُمَا قَوۡلٗا كَرِيمٗا ﴿٢٣﴾ وَٱخۡفِضۡ لَهُمَا جَنَاحَ
ٱلذُّلِّ مِنَ ٱلرَّحۡمَةِ وَقُل رَّبِّ ٱرۡحَمۡهُمَا كَمَا رَبَّيَانِي صَغِيرٗا ﴿٢٤﴾ ﴾

> Your Lord has decreed that you worship none but Him, and that you be kind to parents. Whether one of them or both of them attain old age in your life, say not to them any word of contempt, nor repel them, but address them in terms of honor. And, out of kindness lower to them the wing of humility, and say: "My Lord, bestow on them Your mercy, as

they cherished me in childhood." (Al-Isra' [Night Journey] 17:23–24)

We have an obligation to take care of our children, love them, and raise them well, aware of their duty to serve God. We are also ordered to be good to our neighbors, both in the Qur'an and in the tradition of Prophet Muhammad (PBUH).

﴿ ۞ وَٱعْبُدُوا۟ ٱللَّهَ وَلَا تُشْرِكُوا۟ بِهِۦ شَيْـًٔا ۖ وَبِٱلْوَٰلِدَيْنِ إِحْسَـٰنًا وَبِذِى ٱلْقُرْبَىٰ وَٱلْيَتَـٰمَىٰ وَٱلْمَسَـٰكِينِ
وَٱلْجَارِ ذِى ٱلْقُرْبَىٰ وَٱلْجَارِ ٱلْجُنُبِ وَٱلصَّاحِبِ بِٱلْجَنۢبِ وَٱبْنِ ٱلسَّبِيلِ وَمَا مَلَكَتْ أَيْمَـٰنُكُمْ ۗ إِنَّ ٱللَّهَ
لَا يُحِبُّ مَن كَانَ مُخْتَالًا فَخُورًا ﴿٣٦﴾ ﴾

Serve God, and join not any partners with Him; and do good to parents, kinsfolk, orphans, those in need, neighbors who are kin, and neighbors who are strangers, the companion by your side, the way farer, and what your right hand possess, for God loves not the arrogant, the vainglorious. (An-Nisa' [The Women] 4:36)

Prophet Muhammad (PBUH) gave the advice that we should be good to our neighbors. He said, "Whoever believes in God and the Last Day, let him be good to his neighbor" (narrated by Bukhari). He also said, "Gabriel (the angel of revelation) kept advising me, to be good to my neighbor, that I thought that he will make him inherit me" (narrated by Bukhari).

3

Similarities between the Qur'an and the Bible

In this chapter we will discuss areas and concepts of similarities between the Qur'an and the Bible as it relates to morals and ethics, and to the concept of serving God and our faith.

Morals and Ethics

Both Christians and Muslims believe in moral values and in living their lives guided by ethical standards. We are going to be tested and tried in our lives, and we need to be patient and persevere and never give up hope of God's mercy.

Patience

> Therefore, be patient, brethren, until the coming of the Lord. See how the farmer waits for the precious

fruit of the earth, waiting patiently for it until it receives the early and latter rain. You also be patient, establish your hearts, for the coming of the Lord is at hand. (James 5:7–8)

For whatever things were written before were written for our learning, that we through patience and comfort of the scripture might have hope. (Romans 15:4)

In the Qur'an,

﴿ وَلَنَبْلُوَنَّكُمْ حَتَّىٰ نَعْلَمَ ٱلْمُجَٰهِدِينَ مِنكُمْ وَٱلصَّٰبِرِينَ وَنَبْلُوَا۟ أَخْبَارَكُمْ ﴿٣١﴾ ﴾

And We shall try you until We test those among you who strive their utmost and persevere in patience; and We shall try your reported mettle. (Muhammad [Prophet Muhammad] 47:31)

Those who patiently persevere will get a reward without measure:

إِنَّمَا يُوَفَّى ٱلصَّٰبِرُونَ أَجْرَهُم بِغَيْرِ حِسَابٍ

Those who patiently persevere will truly receive a reward without measure. (Az-Zumar [The Groups] 39:10)

Righteousness

Righteousness is to live our lives conscious of God, not wronging anyone but helping those who need our help and watching our behavior.

> For the Lord is righteous, He loves the righteous, His countenance beholds the upright. (Psalm 11:7)

> The integrity of the upright will guide them, but the perversity of the unfaithful will destroy them. (Proverbs 11:3)

And in the Qur'an, Muslims are ordered to fear God and be conscious of Him.

﴿ يَٰٓأَيُّهَا ٱلَّذِينَ ءَامَنُوا۟ ٱتَّقُوا۟ ٱللَّهَ وَلْتَنظُرْ نَفْسٌ مَّا قَدَّمَتْ لِغَدٍ ۖ وَٱتَّقُوا۟ ٱللَّهَ ۚ إِنَّ ٱللَّهَ خَبِيرٌۢ بِمَا تَعْمَلُونَ ﴿١٨﴾ ﴾

> O you who believe fear God, and let every soul look to what it has sent forth for the morrow; yes fear God, for God is well-acquainted with all that you do. (Al-Hashr [The Gathering] 59:18)

Those who are righteous are close to God and beloved by Him.

﴿ بَلَىٰ مَنْ أَوْفَىٰ بِعَهْدِهِۦ وَٱتَّقَىٰ فَإِنَّ ٱللَّهَ يُحِبُّ ٱلْمُتَّقِينَ ﴿٧٦﴾ ﴾

No, those that keep their plighted faith and act right, indeed God loves those who act right. (Al-Imran [The Family of Imran] 3:76)

The sins of the righteous will be forgiven, and they will be rewarded according to the best of their actions.

﴿ لَهُم مَّا يَشَآءُونَ عِندَ رَبِّهِمْۚ ذَٰلِكَ جَزَآءُ ٱلْمُحْسِنِينَ ﴿٣٤﴾ لِيُكَفِّرَ ٱللَّهُ عَنْهُمْ أَسْوَأَ ٱلَّذِى عَمِلُوا۟
وَيَجْزِيَهُمْ أَجْرَهُم بِأَحْسَنِ ٱلَّذِى كَانُوا۟ يَعْمَلُونَ ﴿٣٥﴾ ﴾

They shall have all that they wish for with their Lord; such is the reward of those who do deeds. So that God will remit from them the worst in their deeds, and give them their reward according to the best of what they have done. (Az-Zumar [The Groups] 39:34–35)

Obedience

We are told to obey God and to be committed to Him and serve Him with devotion.

If you love me keep my commandments. (John 14:15)

For as by one man's disobedience many were made sinners, so also by one man's obedience many will be made righteous. (Romans 5:19)

God is spirit, and those who worship Him must worship Him in spirit and truth. (John 4: 24)

But Peter and the other apostles answered and said: "We ought to obey God rather than men." (Acts 5:29)

And in the Qur'an,

﴿إِنَّمَا كَانَ قَوْلَ ٱلْمُؤْمِنِينَ إِذَا دُعُوٓا۟ إِلَى ٱللَّهِ وَرَسُولِهِۦ لِيَحْكُمَ بَيْنَهُمْ أَن يَقُولُوا۟ سَمِعْنَا وَأَطَعْنَا وَأُو۟لَٰٓئِكَ هُمُ ٱلْمُفْلِحُونَ ﴿٥١﴾﴾

The answer of the believers, when summoned to God and His messenger, in order that he may judge between them, is no other than this: they say: "We hear and we obey". It is such as these that will attain felicity. (An-Nur [The Light] 24:51)

﴿يَٰٓأَيُّهَا ٱلَّذِينَ ءَامَنُوٓا۟ أَطِيعُوا۟ ٱللَّهَ وَأَطِيعُوا۟ ٱلرَّسُولَ وَأُو۟لِى ٱلْأَمْرِ مِنكُمْ

O you who believe obey God, and obey the messenger, and those charged with authority among you. (An-Nisa' [The Women] 4:59)

﴿قُلِ ٱللَّهَ أَعْبُدُ مُخْلِصًا لَّهُۥ دِينِى ﴿١٤﴾﴾

Say: "It is God I serve, with my sincere devotion." (Az-Zumar [The Groups] 39:14)

Humility

Both Christians and Muslims value humility and not looking down at others or behaving in an arrogant way.

> Associate with the humble. Do not be wise in your own opinion. Repay no one evil for evil. Have regards for good things in the sight of all me. If it is possible, as much as depends on you, live peaceably with all men. (Romans 12:16–18)

> Let nothing be done through selfish ambition or conceit, but in lowliness of mind let each esteem others better than himself. Let each of you look out not only for his own interests but also for the interests of others. (Philippians 2:3–4)

> God resists the proud but gives peace to the humble. (James 4:6)

> Humble yourselves in the sight of the Lord, He will lift you up. (James 4:10)

Prophet Muhammad (PBUH) said,

> Charity never decreases your wealth; and whenever a person forgives others, God will raise him in dignity; and whoever humbles himself to God, God will raise him in honor. (Narrated by Ahmad and Muslim)

In the Qur'an,

﴿ يَٰٓأَيُّهَا ٱلَّذِينَ ءَامَنُواْ لَا يَسۡخَرۡ قَوۡمٞ مِّن قَوۡمٍ عَسَىٰٓ أَن يَكُونُواْ خَيۡرٗا مِّنۡهُمۡ وَلَا نِسَآءٞ مِّن نِّسَآءٍ عَسَىٰٓ
أَن يَكُنَّ خَيۡرٗا مِّنۡهُنَّۖ وَلَا تَلۡمِزُوٓاْ أَنفُسَكُمۡ وَلَا تَنَابَزُواْ بِٱلۡأَلۡقَٰبِۖ بِئۡسَ ٱلِٱسۡمُ ٱلۡفُسُوقُ بَعۡدَ ٱلۡإِيمَٰنِۚ
وَمَن لَّمۡ يَتُبۡ فَأُوْلَٰٓئِكَ هُمُ ٱلظَّٰلِمُونَ ١١ ﴾

> O you who believe, let not some men among you laugh at others, it may be that the latter are better than the former; nor let some women laugh at others, it may be that the latter are better than the former; nor defame or be sarcastic to each other, nor call each other by offensive nicknames; ill-seeming is a name connoting wickedness, after he has believed; and those who do not desist are indeed wrong-doers. (Al-Hujurat [The Apartments] 49:11)

Prophet Muhammad (PBUH) said, "None of you will attain faith until he loves for his brother what he loves for himself" (narrated by Bukhari and Muslim).

Mercy and Forgiveness

As God is forgiving, we too should forgive the mistakes of others and be kind and merciful.

> Blessed are the merciful for they shall obtain mercy. (Mathew 5:7)

> Then Peter came to him, and said: "Lord, how often shall my brother sin against me, and I forgive him? Up to seven times?" Jesus said to him, "I do not say to you, up to seven times, but up to seventy times seven." (Mathew 18:21–22)

The Qur'an orders Muslims to forgive and promises God's forgiveness in return.

﴿ وَلْيَعْفُوا۟ وَلْيَصْفَحُوٓا۟ ۗ أَلَا تُحِبُّونَ أَن يَغْفِرَ ٱللَّهُ لَكُمْ ۗ وَٱللَّهُ غَفُورٌ رَّحِيمٌ ﴿٢٢﴾ ﴾

> Let them forgive and overlook, do you not wish that God should forgive you? For God is often-forgiving, most-merciful. (An-Nur [The Light] 24:22)

Knowledge and Understanding

Both Christians and Muslims value knowledge, proper understanding, and critical thinking. Faith based on true knowledge and proper understanding is strong and not easily shaken by adversity.

> Teach me good judgment and knowledge, for I believe Your commandments. (Psalms 119:66)

> To know wisdom and instruction. To perceive the words of understanding. To receive the instruction of wisdom, justice, judgment and equity. To give prudence to the simple, to the young man knowledge

and discretion. A wise man will hear and increase learning, and a man of understanding will attain wise counsel. (Proverbs 1:2–5)

In the Qur’an, the prophet is ordered to seek further knowledge.

﴿ وَقُل رَّبِّ زِدْنِي عِلْمًا ﴿١١٤﴾ ﴾

But say: “My Lord! Advance me in knowledge.” (Taha 20:114)

The Qur’an explains that those who know and understand are not equal to those who are ignorant. Those who know will be reminded of their duty and will fear God.

﴿ أَمَّنْ هُوَ قَٰنِتٌ ءَانَآءَ ٱلَّيْلِ سَاجِدًا وَقَآئِمًا يَحْذَرُ ٱلْءَاخِرَةَ وَيَرْجُوا۟ رَحْمَةَ رَبِّهِۦ ۗ قُلْ هَلْ يَسْتَوِى
ٱلَّذِينَ يَعْلَمُونَ وَٱلَّذِينَ لَا يَعْلَمُونَ ۗ إِنَّمَا يَتَذَكَّرُ أُو۟لُوا۟ ٱلْأَلْبَٰبِ ﴿٩﴾ ﴾

Is one who worships devoutly during the hours of the night, prostrating himself or standing in adoration, who takes heed of the Hereafter, and who places his hope in the mercy of his Lord (like one who does not)? Say: “Are those equal, those who know and those who do not know?” It is those of understanding that receive admonition.” (Az-Zumar [The Groups] 39:9)

إِنَّمَا يَخْشَى ٱللَّهَ مِنْ عِبَادِهِ ٱلْعُلَمَـٰٓؤُا۟

Those truly fear God, among his servants, who have knowledge. (Fatir [Originator] 35:28)

Charity

Charity is a crucial concept both in Christianity and Islam.

> Give to everyone who asks of you. And from him who takes away your goods do not ask them back. And just as you want men to do to you, you also do to them likewise. (Luke 6:30–31)

> But love your enemies, do good and lend, hoping for nothing in return; and your reward will be great, and you will be sons of the Most High. For He is gracious to the ungrateful and evil. (Luke 6:36)

> Each person should do as he has decided in his heart, not out of regret or out of necessity, for God loves a cheerful giver. And God is able to make every grace overflow to you, so that in every way, always having everything you need, you may excel in every good work. (2 Corinthians 9:7–8)

The Qur'an teaches us that God is the real owner and that we have only temporary custody, for we cannot take our money or possessions with us. Therefore, we should help those who are poor and needy.

﴿ وَمَا لَكُمْ أَلَّا تُنفِقُوا فِي سَبِيلِ اللَّهِ وَلِلَّهِ مِيرَاثُ السَّمَاوَاتِ وَالْأَرْضِ ﴾

> Why do you not spend in the cause of God? For to God belongs the heritage of the heavens and the earth. (Al-Hadid [The Iron] 57:10)

﴿ أَوَلَمْ يَرَوْا أَنَّ اللَّهَ يَبْسُطُ الرِّزْقَ لِمَن يَشَاءُ وَيَقْدِرُ ۚ إِنَّ فِي ذَٰلِكَ لَآيَاتٍ لِّقَوْمٍ يُؤْمِنُونَ ﴿٣٧﴾ فَآتِ
ذَا الْقُرْبَىٰ حَقَّهُ وَالْمِسْكِينَ وَابْنَ السَّبِيلِ ۚ ذَٰلِكَ خَيْرٌ لِّلَّذِينَ يُرِيدُونَ وَجْهَ اللَّهِ ۖ وَأُولَٰئِكَ هُمُ
الْمُفْلِحُونَ ﴿٣٨﴾ ﴾

> Do they not see that God enlarges the provision and restricts it, to whomsoever He pleases? Indeed in that are signs for those who believe. So give what is due to kindred, the needy, and the wayfarer. That is best for those who seek the countenance of God, and it is they who will prosper. (Ar-Rum [The Romans] 30: 37–38)

There are ethics in giving charity—in particular, not offending those receiving our charity. Otherwise, our charity is not accepted by God. Also, giving charity in secret is better, for it is not praise or recognition that we seek but to help those who need our help. The Bible explains this concept.

But when you give to the poor, do not let your left hand know what your right hand is doing, so that your giving may be in secret, and your Father who sees you in secret may reward you. (Mathew 6:3)

The Qur'an confirms the concept that we should not give charity in a way that harms those receiving it; otherwise, our charity is not accepted.

﴿ يَٰٓأَيُّهَا ٱلَّذِينَ ءَامَنُوا۟ لَا تُبْطِلُوا۟ صَدَقَٰتِكُم بِٱلْمَنِّ وَٱلْأَذَىٰ كَٱلَّذِى يُنفِقُ مَالَهُۥ رِئَآءَ ٱلنَّاسِ وَلَا يُؤْمِنُ بِٱللَّهِ وَٱلْيَوْمِ ٱلْءَاخِرِ

O you who believe cancel not your charity by reminders of your generosity or by injury, like those who spend their wealth to be seen by men, but believe not in God nor in the Last Day. (Al-Baqara [The Cow] 2:264)

Sometimes giving charity in public is allowed if we want to set an example and encourage others to follow our initiative. But most of the time, it is better to give charity in secret and make sure it reaches those who need it.

﴿ إِن تُبْدُوا۟ ٱلصَّدَقَٰتِ فَنِعِمَّا هِىَ ۖ وَإِن تُخْفُوهَا وَتُؤْتُوهَا ٱلْفُقَرَآءَ فَهُوَ خَيْرٌ لَّكُمْ ۚ وَيُكَفِّرُ عَنكُم مِّن سَيِّـَٔاتِكُمْ ۗ وَٱللَّهُ بِمَا تَعْمَلُونَ خَبِيرٌ ﴿٢٧١﴾ ﴾

If you disclose charity, even so it is well, but if you conceal them, and make them reach those in need, that is best for you; it will remove from you some of your evil; and God is well-acquainted with all that you do. (Al-Baqara [The Cow] 2:271)

Charity is more than just giving money to the poor and needy. Everyone can give charity even if he is poor. The effort that we exert in helping others is a charity. The kind words that we say, the advice that we give, and the example that we set are all kinds of charity if our goal is to help. Even not harming others is considered a charity.

Working and Being Productive

Both Islam and Christianity encourage us to work hard and be productive and hasten in all good deeds. The Qur'an states,

﴿ وَقُلِ ٱعۡمَلُواْ فَسَيَرَى ٱللَّهُ عَمَلَكُمۡ وَرَسُولُهُۥ وَٱلۡمُؤۡمِنُونَۖ

Say: "work righteousness: soon will God observe your work, and his messenger, and the believers." (At-Tawba [Repentance] 9:104)

These good deeds involve many things, which are done to make life better for others, such as feeding the hungry, providing shelter for the homeless, consoling the sufferer, and guiding those who have strayed.

For I was hungry and you gave me food; I was thirsty and you gave me drink; I was a stranger and you took me in; I was naked and you clothed me: I was sick and you visited me; I was in prison and you came to me. Then the righteous will say: "When did we see you hungry and fed you, or thirsty and gave you drink? When did we see you a stranger and took you in, and naked and clothed you? Or when did we see you sick or in prison and came to you? And the King will answer: "Assuredly I say to you, in as much as you did it to one of the least of these my brethren, you did it to me." (Mathew 25:35–40)

Those who have faith acknowledge God's blessings and understand their responsibility in reaching out and helping others. Therefore, they hasten in all good works and are foremost in them.

﴿ وَٱلَّذِينَ يُؤْتُونَ مَآ ءَاتَوا۟ وَّقُلُوبُهُمْ وَجِلَةٌ أَنَّهُمْ إِلَىٰ رَبِّهِمْ رَٰجِعُونَ ﴿٦٠﴾ أُو۟لَٰٓئِكَ يُسَٰرِعُونَ فِى ٱلْخَيْرَٰتِ وَهُمْ لَهَا سَٰبِقُونَ ﴿٦١﴾ ﴾

Those who approach everything that they do with the understanding that they will be brought back to their Lord. Such are the ones who hasten in all good works, and are foremost in them. (Al-Mumenoon [The Believers] 23:60–61)

The Concept of Faith and Serving God

Both Christians and Muslims believe in God and in being accountable to Him. In other words, accountability is a major concept in both religions. The presence of heaven and hell, reward and punishment, and how to achieve salvation are discussed in the Bible and in the Qur'an.

> So it will be at the end of the age. The angels will come forth, separate the wicked from among the just, and cast them into the furnace of fire. There will be wailing and gnashing of teeth. (Mathew 13:49–50)

In the Qur'an the evildoers are contrasted with the righteous. Each gets his reward according to his action.

﴿ ثُمَّ أَوْرَثْنَا ٱلْكِتَٰبَ ٱلَّذِينَ ٱصْطَفَيْنَا مِنْ عِبَادِنَا ۖ فَمِنْهُمْ ظَالِمٌ لِّنَفْسِهِۦ وَمِنْهُم مُّقْتَصِدٌ وَمِنْهُمْ
سَابِقٌۢ بِٱلْخَيْرَٰتِ بِإِذْنِ ٱللَّهِ ۚ ذَٰلِكَ هُوَ ٱلْفَضْلُ ٱلْكَبِيرُ ﴿٣٢﴾

> Then we allowed our servants, whom We have chosen, to inherit the Book; among them are those who wrong themselves, and those who follow a middle course, and those who are foremost in good deeds; this is the greatest blessing. (Fatir [Originator] 35:32)

As to the righteous, they will enter paradise to enjoy.

﴿ جَنَّٰتُ عَدۡنٖ يَدۡخُلُونَهَا يُحَلَّوۡنَ فِيهَا مِنۡ أَسَاوِرَ مِن ذَهَبٖ وَلُؤۡلُؤٗاۖ وَلِبَاسُهُمۡ فِيهَا حَرِيرٞ ﴿٣٣﴾ وَقَالُواْ
ٱلۡحَمۡدُ لِلَّهِ ٱلَّذِيٓ أَذۡهَبَ عَنَّا ٱلۡحَزَنَۖ إِنَّ رَبَّنَا لَغَفُورٞ شَكُورٌ ﴿٣٤﴾ ﴾

> Gardens of eternity they will enter: therein they will be adorned with bracelets of gold and pearls, and their garments will be of silk. And they will say: "Praise be to God who has removed from us all sorrow, for our Lord is indeed often-forgiving, ready to appreciate service." Fatir [Originator] 35:33–34)

As to the wicked who reject faith, they will be in the fire, suffering.

فَٱلَّذِينَ كَفَرُواْ قُطِّعَتۡ لَهُمۡ ثِيَابٞ مِّن نَّارٖ يُصَبُّ مِن فَوۡقِ رُءُوسِهِمُ ٱلۡحَمِيمُ ﴿١٩﴾ يُصۡهَرُ بِهِۦ مَا فِي
بُطُونِهِمۡ وَٱلۡجُلُودُ

> Those who rejected faith, for them will be cut out a garment of fire; over their heads will be poured out boiling water. With it will be melted what is within their bodies, as well as their skins. (Al-Hajj [Pilgrimage] 22:19–20)

We are reminded to be conscious of God, for God knows all that we do, and to prepare for our accountability.

﴿ يَٰٓأَيُّهَا ٱلَّذِينَ ءَامَنُواْ ٱتَّقُواْ ٱللَّهَ وَلۡتَنظُرۡ نَفۡسٞ مَّا قَدَّمَتۡ لِغَدٖۖ وَٱتَّقُواْ ٱللَّهَۚ إِنَّ ٱللَّهَ خَبِيرُۢ بِمَا
تَعۡمَلُونَ ﴿١٨﴾ ﴾

> O you who believe fear God, and let every soul look to what provision he has sent for the morrow, fear God, for God is well-acquainted with all that you do." (Al-Hashr [The Gathering] 59:18)

The Concept of Forgiveness of Sin

The concept of forgiveness of sin has similarities and differences in Christianity and in Islam. In Christianity, forgiveness of sin is a gift from God, obtained by faith in Jesus Christ, for he atoned for the sins of mankind through his sacrifice. "If you confess with your mouth 'Jesus is Lord', and believe in your heart that God raised him from the dead, you will be saved" (Romans 10:10).

In Islam, God is often forgiving, most merciful, but we need to turn to Him and seek His forgiveness. We also need to confirm our faith and do good to wipe out the wrong that we have done. The Qur'an tells us never to despair of the mercy of God.

﴿ ۞ قُلْ يَٰعِبَادِىَ ٱلَّذِينَ أَسْرَفُوا۟ عَلَىٰٓ أَنفُسِهِمْ لَا تَقْنَطُوا۟ مِن رَّحْمَةِ ٱللَّهِ ۚ إِنَّ ٱللَّهَ يَغْفِرُ ٱلذُّنُوبَ جَمِيعًا ۚ إِنَّهُۥ هُوَ ٱلْغَفُورُ ٱلرَّحِيمُ ﴿٥٣﴾ ﴾

> Say: "O my servants who have transgressed against their souls, despair not of the mercy of God, for God forgives all sins; for He is often-forgiving, most-merciful." (Az-Zumar [The Groups] 39:53)

Family Values

Both Christians and Muslims believe in family values and in being good to our neighbors, as we discussed before.

4

Differences Between the Qur'an and the Bible

Divinity of Jesus Christ

The major difference concerns the divinity of Jesus Christ. We will contrast these concepts with verses from the Bible and the Qur'an to illustrate what Christians believe in and how Muslims differ with them.

Christians believe that Jesus is divine and is the son of God and that he came to atone for the sins of the world and gave his life for that reason.

> And I have seen and testified that this is the son of God. (John 1:35)

> But Peter said: "We have come to believe and know that you are the Christ, the son of the living God." (John 6:66)

Simon Peter answered and said: "You are the Christ, the son of the living God." (Mathew 16:6)

Suddenly a voice came out of the cloud, saying: "This is my beloved son, in whom I am well pleased, hear him." (Mathew 17:5)

The Holy Spirit will come upon you, and the power of the highest will overshadow you, therefore, also that Holy One who is to be born will be called the Son of God. (Luke 1:35)

The Qur'an is very clear that Jesus Christ was human and not divine. The Qur'an stresses that both Jesus and Mary were human beings who had to eat their daily bread.

﴿ مَّا ٱلْمَسِيحُ ٱبْنُ مَرْيَمَ إِلَّا رَسُولٌ قَدْ خَلَتْ مِن قَبْلِهِ ٱلرُّسُلُ وَأُمُّهُۥ صِدِّيقَةٌ ۖ كَانَا يَأْكُلَانِ
ٱلطَّعَامَ ۗ ٱنظُرْ كَيْفَ نُبَيِّنُ لَهُمُ ٱلْـَٔايَـٰتِ ثُمَّ ٱنظُرْ أَنَّىٰ يُؤْفَكُونَ ﴿٧٥﴾ ﴾

Christ, the son of Mary, was no more than a messenger, many were the messengers that passed away before him. His mother was a woman of truth. They had both to eat their daily food. See how God does make His signs clear to them; yet see in what ways they are deluded away from the truth! (Al-Maidah [The Table] 5:75)

The Qur'an states that Jesus, the son of Mary, was only a servant of God.

﴿ إِنْ هُوَ إِلَّا عَبْدٌ أَنْعَمْنَا عَلَيْهِ وَجَعَلْنَٰهُ مَثَلًا لِّبَنِيٓ إِسْرَٰٓءِيلَ ﴿٥٩﴾ ﴾

> He was no more than a servant: We granted Our favor to him, and We made him an example to the Children of Israel. (Az-Zukhruf [Gold Adornments] 43:59)

The divinity of Jesus is denied in the Qur'an.

﴿ لَقَدْ كَفَرَ ٱلَّذِينَ قَالُوٓاْ إِنَّ ٱللَّهَ هُوَ ٱلْمَسِيحُ ٱبْنُ مَرْيَمَ ۖ وَقَالَ ٱلْمَسِيحُ يَٰبَنِيٓ إِسْرَٰٓءِيلَ
ٱعْبُدُواْ ٱللَّهَ رَبِّي وَرَبَّكُمْ ۖ إِنَّهُۥ مَن يُشْرِكْ بِٱللَّهِ فَقَدْ حَرَّمَ ٱللَّهُ عَلَيْهِ ٱلْجَنَّةَ وَمَأْوَىٰهُ ٱلنَّارُ ۖ وَمَا
لِلظَّٰلِمِينَ مِنْ أَنصَارٍ ﴿٧٢﴾ ﴾

> They do blaspheme who say: "God is Christ the son of Mary." But said Christ: 'O Children of Israel worship God my Lord and your Lord." Whoever joins other gods with God, God will forbid him the Garden, and the Fire will be his abode. There will for the wrong-doers be no one to help." (Al-Maidah [The Table] 5:72)

The Qur'an states that Jesus never claimed that he was God or the son of God. Rather, he instructed his people to worship the *one* and *only* God, his Lord and their Lord.

﴿ وَإِذْ قَالَ ٱللَّهُ يَٰعِيسَى ٱبْنَ مَرْيَمَ ءَأَنتَ قُلْتَ لِلنَّاسِ ٱتَّخِذُونِى وَأُمِّىَ إِلَٰهَيْنِ مِن دُونِ ٱللَّهِ ۖ قَالَ
سُبْحَٰنَكَ مَا يَكُونُ لِىٓ أَنْ أَقُولَ مَا لَيْسَ لِى بِحَقٍّ ۚ إِن كُنتُ قُلْتُهُۥ فَقَدْ عَلِمْتَهُۥ ۚ تَعْلَمُ مَا فِى نَفْسِى
وَلَآ أَعْلَمُ مَا فِى نَفْسِكَ ۚ إِنَّكَ أَنتَ عَلَّٰمُ ٱلْغُيُوبِ ﴿١١٦﴾ مَا قُلْتُ لَهُمْ إِلَّا مَآ أَمَرْتَنِى بِهِۦٓ أَنِ ٱعْبُدُوا۟
ٱللَّهَ رَبِّى وَرَبَّكُمْ ۚ وَكُنتُ عَلَيْهِمْ شَهِيدًا مَّا دُمْتُ فِيهِمْ ۖ فَلَمَّا تَوَفَّيْتَنِى كُنتَ أَنتَ ٱلرَّقِيبَ عَلَيْهِمْ ۚ وَأَنتَ
عَلَىٰ كُلِّ شَىْءٍ شَهِيدٌ ﴿١١٧﴾ ﴾

> And behold! God will say: "O Jesus the son of Mary! Did you say unto men, "Worship me and my mother as gods in derogation to God?" He will say: "Glory be to You! Never could I say what I had no right (to say). Had I said such a thing, You would indeed have known it. You know what is in my heart, though I know not what is in Yours. For You know in full all that is hidden. Never said I to them aught except what You did command me to say, to wit, "Worship God, my Lord and your Lord"; and I was a witness over them while I dwelt amongst them; when You did take me up You were the watcher over them, and You are a witness to all things." (Al-Maidah [The Table] 5:116–117)

Christians also believe that Jesus Christ was crucified and died on the cross to atone for the sins of man.

> And when Jesus had cried out with a loud voice, he said, "Father, into Your hands I commit My spirit" Having said this, he breathed his last." (Luke 23:46)

> Then they crucified him and divided his garments casting lots. (Mathew 27:35)

> And Jesus cried out with a loud voice, and yielded up His spirit. (Mathew 27:50)

The Qur'an states that Jesus was not crucified, nor did he die on the cross, but a likeness of him appeared to those who saw him.

﴿ وَقَوۡلِهِمۡ إِنَّا قَتَلۡنَا ٱلۡمَسِيحَ عِيسَى ٱبۡنَ مَرۡيَمَ رَسُولَ ٱللَّهِ وَمَا قَتَلُوهُ وَمَا صَلَبُوهُ وَلَٰكِن شُبِّهَ لَهُمۡۚ
وَإِنَّ ٱلَّذِينَ ٱخۡتَلَفُواْ فِيهِ لَفِي شَكّٖ مِّنۡهُۚ مَا لَهُم بِهِۦ مِنۡ عِلۡمٍ إِلَّا ٱتِّبَاعَ ٱلظَّنِّۚ وَمَا قَتَلُوهُ يَقِينَۢا ﴿١٥٧﴾
بَل رَّفَعَهُ ٱللَّهُ إِلَيۡهِۚ وَكَانَ ٱللَّهُ عَزِيزًا حَكِيمٗا ﴿١٥٨﴾ ﴾

> That they said, "We killed Christ Jesus the son of Mary, the messenger of God"; but they killed him not, nor crucified him, but it was made to appear to them, and those who differ are full of doubts, with no certain knowledge, but only conjecture to follow, for a surety they killed him not. No, God raised him up to Himself; and God is exalted in power, wise. (An-Nisa' [The Women] 4:157–158)

Christians believe that Jesus was born through the Holy Spirit, not through normal human contact.

> An angel of the Lord appeared to him in a dream saying: "Joseph the son of David, do not be afraid to

> take to you Mary your wife, for that which is conceived in her is of the Holy Spirit. And she will bring forth a son, and you shall call his name Jesus, for he will save his people from their sins." (Mathew 1:20–21)

> Then Mary said to the angel, "How can this be since I do not know a man?" And the angel answered and said to her, "The Holy Spirit will come upon you, and the power of the Highest will overshadow you; therefore, also, that Holy One who is to be born will be called the Son of God." (Mark 16:34–35)

In the Christian doctrine of the Trinity, the Holy Spirit is one of the three manifestations of God, along with the Father and the Son. In the Qur'an, the Holy Spirit refers to the angel of revelation, Gabriel. He brought God's revelation, namely the Qur'an, to Prophet Muhammad (PBUH).

﴿ وَإِنَّهُۥ لَتَنزِيلُ رَبِّ ٱلْعَـٰلَمِينَ ﴿١٩٢﴾ نَزَلَ بِهِ ٱلرُّوحُ ٱلْأَمِينُ ﴿١٩٣﴾ عَلَىٰ قَلْبِكَ لِتَكُونَ مِنَ ٱلْمُنذِرِينَ ﴿١٩٤﴾ ﴾

> Indeed it is a revelation from the Lord of the worlds. With it came down the Truthful Spirit, to your heart that you may admonish. (Ash-Shura'a [The Poets] 26:192-194)

The same angel strengthened Jesus Christ, God's prophet.

وَءَاتَيْنَا عِيسَى ٱبْنَ مَرْيَمَ ٱلْبَيِّنَٰتِ وَأَيَّدْنَٰهُ بِرُوحِ ٱلْقُدُسِ

> To Jesus the son of Mary We gave clear signs, and strengthened him with the Holy Spirit. (Al-Baqara [The Cow] 2:253)

The Qur'an confirms that Jesus was born from a mother but no father. God can create what He wants. The angel answered Mary's question: how can she have a son when she has no contact with a man?

﴿ قَالَتْ رَبِّ أَنَّىٰ يَكُونُ لِى وَلَدٌ وَلَمْ يَمْسَسْنِى بَشَرٌ ۖ قَالَ كَذَٰلِكِ ٱللَّهُ يَخْلُقُ مَا يَشَآءُ ۚ إِذَا قَضَىٰٓ أَمْرًا فَإِنَّمَا يَقُولُ لَهُۥ كُن فَيَكُونُ ﴿٤٧﴾ ﴾

> She said: "My Lord how shall I have a son when no man has touched me?" He said: "Even so; God created what He wills: when He has decreed a matter, He but says: "Be, and it is." (Al-Imran [The Family of Imran] 3:47)

Salvation in Christianity and in Islam

Both religions believe in heaven and hell, and that as human beings we will be rewarded or punished by God according to our deeds and our sincerity of faith. Those who do good deeds and are righteous will be rewarded in heaven whereas those who are wicked and evil and reject faith will be punished in hell. We need God's mercy and grace to enter heaven because our good deeds alone are not enough. Prophet Muhammad (PBUH) said,

> "None of you, his deeds alone will allow him to enter paradise." His companions asked: "Not even you O Messenger of God?" He said: "Not even I unless God encompasses me in His mercy." (Narrated by Bukhari and Muslim)
>
> But Christians believe that salvation occurs through Jesus Christ. For one to be saved, he must believe in Jesus and that Jesus died on the cross to atone for the sins of mankind. The New Testament states,
>
> And he brought them out and said: "Sirs, what must I do to be saved?" So they said "Believe on the Lord Jesus Christ, and you will be saved, you and your household." (Acts 16:30–31)
>
> For the wages of sin is death. But the gift of God is eternal life in Christ Jesus our Lord. (Romans 6:23)
>
> That if you confess with your mouth the Lord Jesus, and believe in your heart that God has raised him from the dead, you will be saved. (Romans 10:9)
>
> And this is the testimony that God has given us eternal life, and this life is His son. (John 5:11)

> For God so loved the world that He gave His only begotten Son, that whoever believes in Him shall not perish but have ever-lasting life. (John 3:16)

> Jesus answered and said to him: "Most assuredly, I say to you unless one is born again, he cannot see the kingdom of God." (John 3:3)

In Islam, Jesus is but a prophet and messenger of God and has no powers of his own. Salvation occurs through God's mercy and through our good deeds and our sincere faith in God.

﴿ يَٰعِبَادِ لَا خَوۡفٌ عَلَيۡكُمُ ٱلۡيَوۡمَ وَلَآ أَنتُمۡ تَحۡزَنُونَ ٦٨ ٱلَّذِينَ ءَامَنُواْ بِـَٔايَٰتِنَا وَكَانُواْ مُسۡلِمِينَ ٦٩ ٱدۡخُلُواْ ٱلۡجَنَّةَ أَنتُمۡ وَأَزۡوَٰجُكُمۡ تُحۡبَرُونَ ٧٠ ﴾

> My devotees! No fear shall be on you that Day, nor shall you grieve. Being those who believed in Our signs and bowed their wills to Us in Islam. Enter you the Garden, you and your wives in rejoicing. (Az-Zukhruf [Gold Adornments] 43:68–70)

Original Sin

The concept of original sin is different in Islam from Christianity. In Christianity, original sin means that every human being is sinful and his sins can only be cleansed through Jesus Christ, who sacrificed himself to atone for the sins of mankind.

In Islam, Adam sinned and disobeyed God, but Adam repented, and God accepted his repentance.

﴿ فَتَلَقَّىٰٓ ءَادَمُ مِن رَّبِّهِۦ كَلِمَٰتٖ فَتَابَ عَلَيۡهِۚ إِنَّهُۥ هُوَ ٱلتَّوَّابُ ٱلرَّحِيمُ ﴾

> Then Adam learned from his Lord words of inspiration, and his Lord turned to him and accepted his repentance, for He is often-returning, most-merciful. (Al-Baqara [The Cow] 2:37)

Prophet Muhammad (PBUH) told us that every newborn is born with a pure innate nature. It is his parents who make him a Jew or a Christian (narrated by Bukhari). We are born free of sin but earn our sins when we disobey God or commit shameful deeds. We do not bear the sins of our fathers or forefathers, for every soul earns what it does.

﴿ مَّنِ ٱهۡتَدَىٰ فَإِنَّمَا يَهۡتَدِي لِنَفۡسِهِۦۖ وَمَن ضَلَّ فَإِنَّمَا يَضِلُّ عَلَيۡهَاۚ وَلَا تَزِرُ وَازِرَةٞ وِزۡرَ أُخۡرَىٰۗ ﴾

> Who receives guidance, receives it for his own benefit; who goes astray does so to his own loss; no bearer of burdens can bear the burden of another. (Al-Isra' [Night Journey] 17:15)

﴿ لَا يُكَلِّفُ ٱللَّهُ نَفۡسًا إِلَّا وُسۡعَهَاۚ لَهَا مَا كَسَبَتۡ وَعَلَيۡهَا مَا ٱكۡتَسَبَتۡۗ ﴾

> On no soul does God place a burden greater than it can bear. It gets every good that it earns, and it suffers every ill that it earns. (Al-Baqara [The Cow] 2:286)

﴿ كُلُّ نَفْسٍ بِمَا كَسَبَتْ رَهِينَةٌ ﴿٣٨﴾ ﴾

Every soul will be in pledge for its deeds. (Al-Muddathir [One Wrapped Up] 74:38)

So we can see that there are genuine differences between Christianity and Islam, particularly regarding the nature of Jesus Christ (PBUH). These differences should be recognized and not glossed over. There are more areas that both religions share and agree upon, like serving God and being accountable to Him, that we live our lives according to morals and ethics, and that we reach out and help our families, our neighbors, and those who need our help. Both Muslims and Christians should have respect for one another, be kind, and work together as what they share is more than what divides them. It is only through mutual understanding and working together that their collective efforts can help solve the problems that face us all, and we can make the world a better place to live in for everyone, Christian and Muslim alike.

5

Misunderstanding the Qur'an

The Qur'an is misunderstood both by non-Muslims and Muslims. Non-Muslims misunderstand the Qur'an out of ignorance of its message and teachings and because some are prejudiced and biased. Muslims misunderstand the Qur'an because they take some verses out of context and do not understand the Qur'an as a whole.

We will discuss some of the common misconceptions about the Qur'an:

1. Muslims hate non-Muslims and want to force others to become Muslims against their will.
2. Only Muslims are allowed into heaven. Non-Muslims will suffer in hell.
3. The Qur'an is not suitable for our times and cannot be applied in a democratic, pleural society.
4. The Qur'an deprives women of their rights and regards them as inferior to men.

Misconception: Muslims Hate Non-Muslims

There is no verse in the Qur'an that tells Muslims to hate non-Muslims. On the contrary, Muslims respect the people of the book because they were given God's revelations and guidance before. But the Qur'an warns Muslims to be aware that there are some, among the people of the book (Jews and Christians), who hate Muslims and wish to harm them.

﴿ يَٰٓأَيُّهَا ٱلَّذِينَ ءَامَنُواْ لَا تَتَّخِذُواْ بِطَانَةً مِّن دُونِكُمۡ لَا يَأۡلُونَكُمۡ خَبَالًا وَدُّواْ مَا عَنِتُّمۡ قَدۡ بَدَتِ
ٱلۡبَغۡضَآءُ مِنۡ أَفۡوَٰهِهِمۡ وَمَا تُخۡفِي صُدُورُهُمۡ أَكۡبَرُۚ قَدۡ بَيَّنَّا لَكُمُ ٱلۡأٓيَٰتِۖ إِن كُنتُمۡ تَعۡقِلُونَ ١١٨
هَٰٓأَنتُمۡ أُوْلَآءِ تُحِبُّونَهُمۡ وَلَا يُحِبُّونَكُمۡ وَتُؤۡمِنُونَ بِٱلۡكِتَٰبِ كُلِّهِۦ وَإِذَا لَقُوكُمۡ قَالُوٓاْ ءَامَنَّا وَإِذَا خَلَوۡاْ
عَضُّواْ عَلَيۡكُمُ ٱلۡأَنَامِلَ مِنَ ٱلۡغَيۡظِۚ قُلۡ مُوتُواْ بِغَيۡظِكُمۡۗ إِنَّ ٱللَّهَ عَلِيمُۢ بِذَاتِ ٱلصُّدُورِ ١١٩ ﴾

> O you who believe take not into your intimacy those outside your ranks; they will not fail to corrupt you; they only desire for you to suffer. Rank hatred has already appeared from their mouths; what their hearts conceal is far worse. We have made plain to you the signs if you only consider. You love them, but they love you not. Though you believe in the whole of the Book, when they meet you, they say: "we believe", but when they are alone, they bite off the tips of their fingers at you in their rage. Say: "perish in your

rage, God knows well all the secrets of the heart." (Al-Imran [The Family of Imran] 3:118–119)

Another verse that, if taken out of context, can lead to wrong interpretation and may result in wrong behavior. This verse relates to the behavior of the Jews. The Jews in Madinah plotted against the Muslims, caused division among Muslim ranks, and collaborated with the hypocrites in Medina and with Muslim enemies. That is why the Qur'an warns Muslims about the Jews' intentions and behavior.

﴿ ۞ لَتَجِدَنَّ أَشَدَّ ٱلنَّاسِ عَدَٰوَةً لِّلَّذِينَ ءَامَنُوا۟ ٱلْيَهُودَ وَٱلَّذِينَ أَشْرَكُوا۟ ۖ وَلَتَجِدَنَّ أَقْرَبَهُم
مَّوَدَّةً لِّلَّذِينَ ءَامَنُوا۟ ٱلَّذِينَ قَالُوٓا۟ إِنَّا نَصَٰرَىٰ ۚ ذَٰلِكَ بِأَنَّ مِنْهُمْ قِسِّيسِينَ وَرُهْبَانًا وَأَنَّهُمْ لَا
يَسْتَكْبِرُونَ ﴿٨٢﴾ ﴾

Strongest in enmity to the believers you will find the Jews and Pagans; and nearest in love to the believers you will find those who say: "We are Christians." Because among them are those devoted to learning and those who have renounced the world, and they are not arrogant." (Al-Maidah [The Table] 5:82)

This verse does not mean that all Jews hate the Muslims or that all Christians love the Muslims. It only represents the situation at the time of Prophet Muhammad (PBUH) in Madinah. Current-day Jews do not bear the sins of their predecessors. Also, many Christians hated the Muslims and waged wars against them.

The Qur'an orders Muslims to treat non-Muslims with kindness and justice, to talk to them in a good way, to work with them and cooperate in virtue, not to prejudge their fate, to respect their right to their faith and convictions, and *not* force them to accept Islam against their will.

As long as non-Muslims are not frank enemies and do not behave in a wrong way, then Muslims are ordered to treat them with kindness and justice.

﴿لَّا يَنْهَىٰكُمُ ٱللَّهُ عَنِ ٱلَّذِينَ لَمْ يُقَٰتِلُوكُمْ فِى ٱلدِّينِ وَلَمْ يُخْرِجُوكُم مِّن دِيَٰرِكُمْ أَن تَبَرُّوهُمْ وَتُقْسِطُوٓا۟
إِلَيْهِمْ ۚ إِنَّ ٱللَّهَ يُحِبُّ ٱلْمُقْسِطِينَ ﴿٨﴾﴾

> God forbids you not, regarding those who fight you not because of your faith nor drive you out of your homes, from treating them with kindness and justice. For God loves those who are just. (Al-Mumtahanah [Woman to Be Examined] 60:8)

Muslims are ordered to talk to others in a good way because Satan incites enmity and hatred and wishes to cause division.

﴿وَقُل لِّعِبَادِى يَقُولُوا۟ ٱلَّتِى هِىَ أَحْسَنُ ۚ إِنَّ ٱلشَّيْطَٰنَ يَنزَغُ بَيْنَهُمْ ۚ إِنَّ ٱلشَّيْطَٰنَ كَانَ لِلْإِنسَٰنِ
عَدُوًّا مُّبِينًا ﴿٥٣﴾﴾

> Tell My servants to say those things that are best, for Satan incites enmity and causes division among them, for Satan is an avowed enemy to man. (Al-Isra' [Night Journey] 17:53)

Muslims are ordered in the Qur'an to cooperate and work with others, to advance virtue and righteousness, but not to collaborate in sin or transgression.

وَتَعَاوَنُوا۟ عَلَى ٱلْبِرِّ وَٱلتَّقْوَىٰ ۖ وَلَا تَعَاوَنُوا۟ عَلَى ٱلْإِثْمِ وَٱلْعُدْوَٰنِ ۚ وَٱتَّقُوا۟ ٱللَّهَ ۖ

> And work together in virtue and righteousness, but not in sin or transgression, and fear God. (Al-Maidah [The Table] 5:2)

Muslims are told not to prejudge the fate of others. The order came to Prophet Muhammad (PBUH) to do his job and deliver God's message and not to worry about the fate of those who reject faith because their account is with God.

فَإِنَّمَا عَلَيْكَ ٱلْبَلَٰغُ وَعَلَيْنَا ٱلْحِسَابُ

> Your duty is to deliver the message; it is up to Us to hold them accountable. (Ar-Ra'd [The Thunder] 13:40)

Muslims are told that God gave man the right to accept faith or reject faith; hence, man is responsible for his choice and decision and is accountable to God for his actions.

ﵟفَمَن شَآءَ فَلۡيُؤۡمِن وَمَن شَآءَ فَلۡيَكۡفُرۡﵞ

> Let him who will believe, and let him who will reject faith. (Al-Kahf [The Cave] 18:29)

Therefore, there should be *no* compulsion in religion, for the truth is apparent.

﴿لَآ إِكۡرَاهَ فِي ٱلدِّينِۖ قَد تَّبَيَّنَ ٱلرُّشۡدُ مِنَ ٱلۡغَيِّ﴾

> Let there be no compulsion in religion, truth stands clear from error. (Al-Baqara [The Cow] 2:256)

The order came from God, warning Prophet Muhammad (PBUH) from forcing others to accept Islam against their will.

﴿وَلَوۡ شَآءَ رَبُّكَ لَأٓمَنَ مَن فِي ٱلۡأَرۡضِ كُلُّهُمۡ جَمِيعًاۚ أَفَأَنتَ تُكۡرِهُ ٱلنَّاسَ حَتَّىٰ يَكُونُواْ مُؤۡمِنِينَ ٩٩﴾

> If it was the will of your Lord, then everyone on earth would have believed. Are you then forcing people to believe against their will? (Yunus [Jonah] 10:99)

Some verses in the Qur'an, if taken out of context, can be misunderstood. An example is the following:

﴿ قَٰتِلُوا۟ ٱلَّذِينَ لَا يُؤْمِنُونَ بِٱللَّهِ وَلَا بِٱلْيَوْمِ ٱلْءَاخِرِ وَلَا يُحَرِّمُونَ مَا حَرَّمَ ٱللَّهُ وَرَسُولُهُۥ وَلَا
يَدِينُونَ دِينَ ٱلْحَقِّ مِنَ ٱلَّذِينَ أُوتُوا۟ ٱلْكِتَٰبَ حَتَّىٰ يُعْطُوا۟ ٱلْجِزْيَةَ عَن يَدٍ وَهُمْ صَٰغِرُونَ
﴿٢٩﴾ ﴾

> Fight those who believe not in God or the Last Day, nor hold that forbidden which has been forbidden by God and his messenger, nor acknowledge the religion of truth, from among the people of the Book until they pay the Jizya with willing submission, and feel themselves subdued. (At-Tawbah [Repentance] 9:29)

This verse refers to the Jews who fought the Muslims and the Muslim state in Madinah at the time of Prophet Muhammad (PBUH). They were fierce enemies and plotted with Muslim enemies. The order to fight them was based on their behavior and not because of their faith as Jews. The Qur'an recognizes and respects the faith of both Jews and Christians because their religion came from the same God who sent the Qur'an to Prophet Muhammad (PBUH).

Misconception: Only Muslims Will Enter Heaven

This view is shared by many Muslims because they equate Jews and Christians with rejection of faith and call them *kuffar* (unbelievers). The Qur'an tells us that those who reject faith are the losers and will dwell in hell forever.

﴿إِنَّ ٱلَّذِينَ كَفَرُواْ لَن تُغۡنِيَ عَنۡهُمۡ أَمۡوَٰلُهُمۡ وَلَآ أَوۡلَٰدُهُم مِّنَ ٱللَّهِ شَيۡـٔٗاۖ وَأُوْلَٰٓئِكَ أَصۡحَٰبُ ٱلنَّارِۚ
هُمۡ فِيهَا خَٰلِدُونَ ١١٦﴾

> Those who reject faith, neither their possessions nor their progeny will help them against God at all; they will be companions of the Fire, to dwell therein forever. (Al-Imran [The Family of Imran] 3:116)

The Christians believe in the Trinity; meaning, that God manifests in three forms: the Father, the Son, and the Holy Spirit. Such conviction contradicts the Qur'anic concept that there is only *one* God and that Jesus is human and not divine. The Qur'an refers to the Christians who hold such a belief as having rejected faith. The Jews, as well as the Christians, do not believe in the Qur'an as a divine book and deny that Muhammad is God's messenger.

But the Qur'an also states that among the people of the book are righteous people, who have faith in God and believe in being accountable to Him and who hasten in good, righteous deeds. It also states that their effort is appreciated and not rejected.

﴿۞ لَيۡسُواْ سَوَآءٗۗ مِّنۡ أَهۡلِ ٱلۡكِتَٰبِ أُمَّةٞ قَآئِمَةٞ يَتۡلُونَ ءَايَٰتِ ٱللَّهِ ءَانَآءَ ٱلَّيۡلِ وَهُمۡ يَسۡجُدُونَ ١١٣
يُؤۡمِنُونَ بِٱللَّهِ وَٱلۡيَوۡمِ ٱلۡأٓخِرِ وَيَأۡمُرُونَ بِٱلۡمَعۡرُوفِ وَيَنۡهَوۡنَ عَنِ ٱلۡمُنكَرِ وَيُسَٰرِعُونَ فِي
ٱلۡخَيۡرَٰتِۖ وَأُوْلَٰٓئِكَ مِنَ ٱلصَّٰلِحِينَ ١١٤ وَمَا يَفۡعَلُواْ مِنۡ خَيۡرٖ فَلَن يُكۡفَرُوهُۗ وَٱللَّهُ عَلِيمُۢ بِٱلۡمُتَّقِينَ
١١٥﴾

> Not all of them are alike; of the people of the Book are a portion that stand for the right; they rehearse the signs of God all night long, and prostrate themselves in adoration. They believe in God and in the Last Day; they enjoin what is right, and forbid what is wrong; and they hasten in all good deeds; they are in the ranks of the righteous. Of the good that they do nothing will be rejected of them, for God knows well those who do right. (Al-Imran [The Family of Imran] 3:113–115)

Some hard line Muslims state that those "good" Christians and Jews will get their reward in this life but will have no reward in the hereafter because they did not accept the Qur'an or Prophet Muhammad (PBUH). The Qur'an, however, is clear that anyone who believes in God and in being accountable to God, is righteous, and does good have nothing to fear and will get their reward from God.

﴿ إِنَّ ٱلَّذِينَ ءَامَنُواْ وَٱلَّذِينَ هَادُواْ وَٱلنَّصَٰرَىٰ وَٱلصَّٰبِـِٔينَ مَنْ ءَامَنَ بِٱللَّهِ وَٱلْيَوْمِ ٱلْءَاخِرِ وَعَمِلَ
صَٰلِحًا فَلَهُمْ أَجْرُهُمْ عِندَ رَبِّهِمْ وَلَا خَوْفٌ عَلَيْهِمْ وَلَا هُمْ يَحْزَنُونَ ٦٢ ﴾

> Those who believe, those who follow the Jewish (scripture), and the Sabians and the Christians- any who believe in God and the Last Day, and work righteousness- on them shall be no fear, nor shall they grieve. (Al-Baqara [The Cow] 2:62)

The sincere effort of those who have faith and do righteous deeds is never wasted, as God promised.

﴿ فَمَن يَعۡمَلۡ مِنَ ٱلصَّٰلِحَٰتِ وَهُوَ مُؤۡمِنٞ فَلَا كُفۡرَانَ لِسَعۡيِهِۦ وَإِنَّا لَهُۥ كَٰتِبُونَ ٩٤ ﴾

> Whoever works any acts of righteousness and has faith, his endeavor will not be rejected: We shall record it in his favor. (Al-Anbiya [The Prophets] 21:94)

Moderate Muslims, therefore, believe that God will accept the good, righteous deeds of both Jews and Christians if they have faith in God and believe in being accountable to Him. Their judgment is with their Lord, who is just and will not treat anyone unfairly. To state categorically that non-Muslims are doomed to hellfire does not make sense because some have not heard of Islam or its teachings, and many only have wrong information, which distorts the true teachings of Islam.

Who is then responsible? Those who got distorted information or those who painted this terrible picture of Islam and the Muslims? What matters is faith in God and living our life as decent human beings, doing good and shunning evil—whether that faith corresponds to traditional Islam, another form of religion that came from God, or a code of morals and ethics

Religion is meant to improve our character and behavior and makes us better human beings, more caring and helpful, and more responsible. If our religion does not do that, then we misunderstand the vision and goal of our faith. It is not our prayers or fasting or the way we dress that validates our Islam. Rather, it is our kindness, love for others, and reaching out to help the poor, the needy, and the disadvantaged. If non-Muslims exhibit this behavior, then they are believers, although they are not Muslims. If Muslims are arrogant, unkind, hateful, and un-willing to help those in need, then they have no faith, even if they call themselves Muslims.

Misconception: The Qur'an Is Not Suitable for Our Times

Though the Qur'an was revealed fourteen centuries ago, it is a divine revelation that can be applied in any society because principles of morality and our accountability to God do not change with time or place. To be truthful, to be kind and forgiving, to seek the truth and accept it, to be just, and not to wrong others are applicable whether one lives in the desert or in a highly developed society. Understanding our accountability to God, serving Him by sharing His blessings with the poor, and helping those in need are valid and applicable in any society. These are the core teachings of the Qur'an, and they are valid and applicable today in America as they were 1,400 years ago.

Our understanding of the Qur'an and how to apply its teachings depends on the society we live in. The Qur'an does not restrict us with too many details; therefore, its teachings are applicable at all times. The verse stating that the thief's hand be cut must be understood today in a different way. Nowadays it means that the thief should be punished, but that punishment can change from one society to another, depending on what is more appropriate and accepted. The punishment for adultery nowadays is not stoning. What is important is that both stealing and adultery are wrong and should be avoided, and those committing these major sins need to be punished.

Charging exuberant interest rates that enslave the borrower is wrong. How can we deal with usury is subject to debate. The beauty of the Qur'an is that it gives us the principle and guideline and the rationale and leaves the application to each society, depending on its special circumstances.

The principles of democracy are rooted in the Qur'an. Freedom of thought and expression and faith, and justice and accountability are all Qur'anic principles. The Qur'an safeguards freedom of thought and faith. Muslims are told to respect the right of everyone to decide for themselves what to believe in and that the life and liberties of each human being are to be safeguarded.

Justice is a cardinal concept in the Qur'an for Muslims and non-Muslims alike. The Qur'an orders Muslims to be just and not to allow their likes or dislikes to make them deviate from justice or decline to establish justice.

﴿ ۞ يَـٰٓأَيُّهَا ٱلَّذِينَ ءَامَنُوا۟ كُونُوا۟ قَوَّٰمِينَ بِٱلْقِسْطِ شُهَدَآءَ لِلَّهِ وَلَوْ عَلَىٰٓ أَنفُسِكُمْ أَوِ ٱلْوَٰلِدَيْنِ وَٱلْأَقْرَبِينَ
إِن يَكُنْ غَنِيًّا أَوْ فَقِيرًا فَٱللَّهُ أَوْلَىٰ بِهِمَا ۖ فَلَا تَتَّبِعُوا۟ ٱلْهَوَىٰٓ أَن تَعْدِلُوا۟ ۚ وَإِن تَلْوُۥٓا۟ أَوْ تُعْرِضُوا۟ فَإِنَّ
ٱللَّهَ كَانَ بِمَا تَعْمَلُونَ خَبِيرًا ﴿١٣٥﴾ ﴾

> O you who believe stand up for justice, as witnesses for God, even if it is against your own souls, or parents or kindred; should he be rich or poor, God will take care of both of them. Therefore do not follow your lusts, otherwise you will not be just; and if you turn away or decline to do justice, indeed God is well aware of all that you do. (An-Nisa' [The Women] 4:135)

We are responsible to work to the best of our ability, to be honest, and not to cheat. We are accountable for our actions. Nothing that we do can escape the knowledge of God.

The Qur'an does not specify a certain form of government because what may be appropriate for one society may not be right under different circumstances. What is always right and should be followed under any form of government is that people are free and not oppressed, and that justice is established so that no one is wronged, and there is accountability.

To be able to work, achieve, and enjoy life is stressed in the Qur'an:

Say: "Who has made forbidden the beauty that Allah has made available for His servants, and the good and pure things in life?" (Al-Araf 7: 32)

Such enjoyment should be in moderation and not engaging in what is wrong and unlawful.

Misconception: Women Are Treated as Second-Class Citizens in Muslim Countries and Are Denied Their Rights

Some argue that the Qur'an orders men to beat their wives. This is a wrong understanding of a Qur'anic verse that discusses disorder and quarrels in married life, and prescribes three stages to deal with this problem.

﴿ ٱلرِّجَالُ قَوَّٰمُونَ عَلَى ٱلنِّسَآءِ بِمَا فَضَّلَ ٱللَّهُ بَعۡضَهُمۡ عَلَىٰ بَعۡضٖ وَبِمَآ أَنفَقُواْ مِنۡ أَمۡوَٰلِهِمۡۚ فَٱلصَّٰلِحَٰتُ قَٰنِتَٰتٌ حَٰفِظَٰتٞ لِّلۡغَيۡبِ بِمَا حَفِظَ ٱللَّهُۚ وَٱلَّٰتِي تَخَافُونَ نُشُوزَهُنَّ فَعِظُوهُنَّ وَٱهۡجُرُوهُنَّ فِي ٱلۡمَضَاجِعِ وَٱضۡرِبُوهُنَّۖ فَإِنۡ أَطَعۡنَكُمۡ فَلَا تَبۡغُواْ عَلَيۡهِنَّ سَبِيلًاۗ إِنَّ ٱللَّهَ كَانَ عَلِيّٗا كَبِيرٗا ٣٤ ﴾

> Men are the protectors and maintainers of women, because God has given the one more (strength) than the other, and because they support them from their means. Therefore, the righteous women are devoutly obedient, and guard what God would have them guard. As to those women on whose part you feel disloyalty and ill-conduct, admonish them first,

> next refuse to share their beds, and last beat them (lightly); but if they return to obedience, seek not against them means of annoyance, for God is most-high, great. (An-Nisa' [The Women] 4:34)

The first stage advises and reminds that both spouses have responsibility toward their family and are accountable to God. If this step fails, then the next step is for the husband not to have intimate contact with rebellious wives. This should wake them up. Only rarely, and if the two steps fail, the Qur'an permits light beating, which the prophet explained but did not recommend—rather, did not like. The prophet (PBUH) never beat any of his wives. Therefore, we should understand that wife-beating is not allowed in Islam.

Wife-beating may have had a place in a primitive society, but it has no place in a society that respects the rights of both men and women. The Qur'an explains that the relationship between spouses is based on kindness, love, mercy, and each one finding peace and happiness. How can such a relationship then be disregarded and destroyed by a man beating his wife? This Qur'anic verse is about resolving differences and making sure that lines of communication are kept open between the married couple. How this is applied may differ from one society to another.

Some men misunderstand this verse to mean that the man is better than his wife because God gave him the leadership role in his family. Such a role is one of responsibility, not arrogance or dictatorship. A man is not better than his wife. They compete in faith and righteousness and help each other. They respect and seek each other's opinion before a decision that will affect their family is made. The Qur'an stresses the value of consultation as a characteristic of God's righteous servants.

﴿ وَٱلَّذِينَ ٱسْتَجَابُوا۟ لِرَبِّهِمْ وَأَقَامُوا۟ ٱلصَّلَوٰةَ وَأَمْرُهُمْ شُورَىٰ بَيْنَهُمْ وَمِمَّا رَزَقْنَٰهُمْ يُنفِقُونَ ﴿٣٨﴾ ﴾

> And those who did respond to their Lord, and established regular prayer, and decide their affairs through mutual consultation among themselves, and spend out of what We provided for them. (Ash-Shuraa [Consultation] 42:38)

The Qur'an recognizes the human dignity of both men and women and stresses that no one is superior to another except through righteousness. Each spouse has responsibilities to perform and a role to fulfill. Both man and woman will get his/her reward according to their deeds.

﴿ مَنْ عَمِلَ صَٰلِحًا مِّن ذَكَرٍ أَوْ أُنثَىٰ وَهُوَ مُؤْمِنٌ فَلَنُحْيِيَنَّهُۥ حَيَوٰةً طَيِّبَةً ۖ وَلَنَجْزِيَنَّهُمْ أَجْرَهُم بِأَحْسَنِ مَا كَانُوا۟ يَعْمَلُونَ ﴿٩٧﴾ ﴾

> Whoever works righteousness, man or woman, and has faith, We will let them live a good life, and We will reward them according to the best of their deeds. (An-Nahl [The Bees] 16:97)

If in some Muslim countries women are not given their rights or treated badly, it is against the teachings of the Qur'an, and stems from tribal tradition that has no merit or basis. Worse, in some Muslim countries, girls are not allowed a proper education and are raised only to get married and serve their husbands. To know and understand and learn is a basic right that no human being should be denied. The Qur'an stresses the importance of learning and knowledge and distinguishes between those who know and those who are ignorant.

The Qur'an praises many women, among them are two women noted in chapter 66 of the Qur'an. These are the wife of Pharaoh, who took Moses and raised him, and Marium (Mary), who guarded her chastity and was devout and obedient to God. Prophet Muhammad (PBUH) praised those men who treated their wives well and stated that they are the best. He said, "The best among you, are the best to his wife and family; and among you, I am best to my wife and family" (narrated by Bukhari).

PART II
MUHAMMAD

6

The Life of Muhammad (Seerah)

The Early Years Before the Revelation

Muhammad was born in a noble house in Macca from the tribe of Quraish, which was respected all over Arabia. He was born in the year AD 571. He was an orphan as he lost both his father and mother at an early age. He worked as a shepherd then became a merchant. He was known by two nicknames: Al-Ameen (the one to be trusted) and As-Sadiq (the truthful one). He never prostrated to an idol and did not gamble, drink alcohol, nor commit adultery.

Muhammad is a descendant of Ismail, the son of Ibrahim. Muhammad married Khadija when he was twenty-five years old. She was his only wife for twenty-five years. His two sons died in infancy, and he had four daughters, who all died during his life—except for his youngest daughter, Fatima, who died shortly after his death.

He used to meditate, think, reflect, and search for God. One of his favorite places was a cave at the top of a mountain near Macca called the cave of Hira'. This meditation purified his soul and brought him close to God.

Here are some important lessons:

1. Being born from a noble family and from a famous tribe gave Muhammad respect and distinction among his peers, which would help him later on in his mission as a prophet.
2. Early on he was known for his morals and noble character, and people trusted him and respected him.
3. Through meditation and reflection, his soul was purified and was ready to receive divine guidance.
4. His wife supported him and provided for him a peaceful, happy home. He was faithful to his wife and acknowledged God's blessing.

The Revelation from God

Muhammad was forty years old when the angel Gabriel appeared to him in the cave of Hira'. He ordered him to read verses from the Qur'an. Muhammad was illiterate and said, "I cannot read." The angel recited the first verses of Surat Al-Alaq (The Clot), chapter 96 in the Qur'an:

﴿ ٱقْرَأْ بِٱسْمِ رَبِّكَ ٱلَّذِى خَلَقَ ﴿١﴾ خَلَقَ ٱلْإِنسَٰنَ مِنْ عَلَقٍ ﴿٢﴾ ٱقْرَأْ وَرَبُّكَ ٱلْأَكْرَمُ ﴿٣﴾ ٱلَّذِى عَلَّمَ
بِٱلْقَلَمِ ﴿٤﴾ عَلَّمَ ٱلْإِنسَٰنَ مَا لَمْ يَعْلَمْ ﴿٥﴾ ﴾

> Read in the name of your Lord, Who created man out of a leech-like clot. Read and your Lord is most bountiful. He taught man that which man did not know. (Al-Alaq [The Clot] 96:1–5)

Prophet Muhammad (PBUH) saw the angel in its huge form with wings and returned home frightened. His wife comforted him and reassured him. The Qur'an tells us that Muhammad could not read nor write.

﴿ وَمَا كُنتَ تَتْلُوا۟ مِن قَبْلِهِۦ مِن كِتَٰبٍ وَلَا تَخُطُّهُۥ بِيَمِينِكَ ۖ إِذًا لَّٱرْتَابَ ٱلْمُبْطِلُونَ ﴿٤٨﴾ ﴾

> You were not able to recite a book before this Book came, nor are you able to write it with your right hand. In that case, indeed, would the talkers of vanity have doubted (this Qur'an). (Al-Ankabut [The Spider] 29:48)

Muhammad continued to receive divine revelation for twenty-three years. As we discussed before, the Qur'an came interrupted over many years to solve problems, answer questions, strengthen the heart of the prophet and his companions, and give them time to recite it, memorize it, understand it, and apply its message. The few verses of the Qur'an that were revealed from time to time were written down by a group of the prophet's companions. Another group memorized these verses. The Qur'an is recited in prayer, and this facilitated the process of memorization. Thus the Qur'an was saved both in written and oral forms as God promised to safeguard the Qur'an.

﴿ إِنَّا نَحْنُ نَزَّلْنَا ٱلذِّكْرَ وَإِنَّا لَهُۥ لَحَٰفِظُونَ ۝٩ ﴾

> We have sent down this message, and we will safeguard it. (Al-Hijr [Rocky Tract] 15:9)

The prophet (PBUH) recited the verses of the Qur'an revealed to him, explained it, and applied its teachings and guidelines in his character and behavior. Therefore, he became an example to follow, as the Qur'an explains:

﴿ لَّقَدْ كَانَ لَكُمْ فِى رَسُولِ ٱللَّهِ أُسْوَةٌ حَسَنَةٌ لِّمَن كَانَ يَرْجُوا ٱللَّهَ وَٱلْيَوْمَ ٱلْـَٔاخِرَ وَذَكَرَ ٱللَّهَ كَثِيرًا

۝٢١ ﴾

> You have indeed in the messenger of God a beautiful example of conduct to whom who rests his hopes in meeting God, and the Last Day, and who remembers God often. (Al-Ahzab [The Confederates] 33:21)

The first ones to believe in Muhammad as God's messenger were his wife, his close friends, and his cousin. The early phase of Islam was secret for fear of persecution by the tribe of Quraish, which used to worship idols.

The early Qur'an encouraged patience and perseverance, and it explained the duty of mankind to worship and serve God. It forbid evil and shameful deeds and promised God's reward for righteous conduct. The early Muslims were few but united by their faith.

After three years of secret *da'wa* (calling to Allah), the order came from God to his messenger to proclaim the *da'wa*. Muhammad gathered his clan and told them that he was God's messenger and invited them to worship and serve God. The reaction of Quraish was swift and harsh. They understood that accepting Muhammad's call to God means denouncing their idols, and they feared that the pilgrims who used to come to Mecca to visit the holy shrine would no longer come and they would lose their status as guardians of the *haram* (shrine). The Qur'an explains their fears and refutes it.

﴿ وَقَالُوٓا۟ إِن نَّتَّبِعِ ٱلْهُدَىٰ مَعَكَ نُتَخَطَّفْ مِنْ أَرْضِنَآ ۚ أَوَلَمْ نُمَكِّن لَّهُمْ حَرَمًا ءَامِنًا يُجْبَىٰٓ إِلَيْهِ
ثَمَرَٰتُ كُلِّ شَىْءٍ رِّزْقًا مِّن لَّدُنَّا وَلَٰكِنَّ أَكْثَرَهُمْ لَا يَعْلَمُونَ ﴿٥٧﴾ ﴾

> They say: "If we were to follow the guidance with you, we would be snatched away from our land." Have We not established for them a secure sanctuary to which We brought as tribute all kinds of fruit, a provision from Ourselves? But most of them understand not." (Al-Qasas [The Stories] 28:57)

The Quraish resistance and rejection of Muhammad was based on economic and political reasons. They feared loss of income and leadership positions among the Arabs. The Qur'an explains that they were not rejecting Muhammad but God's message. They knew Muhammad as an honest, truthful person and trusted him, but they did not want their status and way of life to change.

فَإِنَّهُمْ لَا يُكَذِّبُونَكَ وَلَٰكِنَّ ٱلظَّٰلِمِينَ بِـَٔايَٰتِ ٱللَّهِ يَجْحَدُونَ ﴿٣٣﴾

> They are not rejecting you, but it is the signs of God that the wicked deny. (Al-An'am [The Cattle] 6:33)

﴿ بَلْ قَالُوٓا۟ إِنَّا وَجَدْنَآ ءَابَآءَنَا عَلَىٰٓ أُمَّةٍ وَإِنَّا عَلَىٰٓ ءَاثَٰرِهِم مُّهْتَدُونَ ﴿٢٢﴾ ﴾

> They say: "We found our fathers following a certain religion, and we do guide ourselves by their footsteps." (Az-Zukhruf [Gold Adornments] 43:22)

The resistance and rejection of Quraish started by ridiculing Muhammad and his followers. They said that he was insane, a sorcerer, and surely he was lying. They said that his message were only tales of the ancient that he learned.

﴿ وَقَالُوا۟ يَٰٓأَيُّهَا ٱلَّذِى نُزِّلَ عَلَيْهِ ٱلذِّكْرُ إِنَّكَ لَمَجْنُونٌ ﴿٦﴾ ﴾

> They said: "O you to whom the message is being revealed! Truly you are mad or possessed!" (Al-Hijr [Rocky Tract] 15:6)

﴿ وَقَالُوٓا۟ أَسَٰطِيرُ ٱلْأَوَّلِينَ ٱكْتَتَبَهَا فَهِىَ تُمْلَىٰ عَلَيْهِ بُكْرَةً وَأَصِيلًا ﴿٥﴾ ﴾

> They said: "Tales of the ancient, which he has caused to be written and they are dictated to him morning and evening." (Al-Furqan [The Criterion] 25:5)

They tried to disturb and prevent others from listening to the Qur'an as Muhammad was reciting it.

﴿ وَقَالَ ٱلَّذِينَ كَفَرُوا۟ لَا تَسْمَعُوا۟ لِهَٰذَا ٱلْقُرْءَانِ وَٱلْغَوْا۟ فِيهِ لَعَلَّكُمْ تَغْلِبُونَ ﴿٢٦﴾ ﴾

> Those who reject faith say: "Listen not to this Qur'an, but talk at random while it is being recited, that you may gain the upper hand." (Fussilat [Explained in Detail] 41:26)

The Quraish also tried to torture and abuse the weak among the Muslims to make them renounce their faith. Some withstood the torture while others died, but no one renounced their faith.

Muhammad received divine revelation in three ways:

1. Through the angel Gabriel, who related to the prophet God's words
2. Through inspiration to his heart and mind
3. Directly from God, when God talked to him

The Qur'an states,

﴿ ۞ وَمَا كَانَ لِبَشَرٍ أَن يُكَلِّمَهُ ٱللَّهُ إِلَّا وَحْيًا أَوْ مِن وَرَآئِ حِجَابٍ أَوْ يُرْسِلَ رَسُولًا فَيُوحِيَ بِإِذْنِهِۦ

مَا يَشَآءُ ۚ إِنَّهُۥ عَلِيٌّ حَكِيمٌ ﴾ We

> It is not fitting for a man that God should speak to him except by inspiration, or from behind a veil, or by the sending of a messenger to reveal, with God's permission, what God wills, for God is most-high, most-wise. (Ash-Shuraa [The Consultation] 42:51)

We learn the following lessons:

1. Those who reject faith will do anything to distort God's message and prevent others from reaching the truth. They resist social justice and morality, and they want to keep their power and influence. Their methods may change in different societies, but their goal is the same: to defeat the truth and obstruct others from accepting God's message.
2. God made sure that his message is safeguarded and not altered. The Qur'an has been preserved both in written and oral forms. The Arabic Qur'an that we have today is the same Qur'an revealed to Prophet Muhammad (PBUH).
3. God's prophet and the early Muslims faced persecution and abuse, as do all men of faith, and

their message was distorted. But they patiently persevered and continued their call to invite others to God. We cannot be discouraged or give up when we meet rejection and abuse because we are doing God's work, and God will help us in due time

4. The proof of the authenticity of the Qur'an is in the Qur'an itself. We need to know the Qur'an and be able to cite verses from the Qur'an that supports what we say and explains the truth from God. The Qur'an has a profound effect on those willing to listen to its divine message.

The Immigration to Habesha (Ethiopia)

As Muslims in Mecca continued to suffer oppression from Quraish, the prophet (PBUH) gave permission to some Muslims to immigrate to Habesha, saying: "Go to Habesha, where the king is just and wrongs no one, until Allah delivers you from your difficulty."

The first immigration occurred in the fifth year after the revelation. There were twelve men and four women. They were received well by the Christian king named An-Najashi. Quraish tried to influence the king and persuade him to send the Muslim immigrants back to Quraish. He refused till he heard their side of the story. One of the Muslim immigrants explained to the king their plight and that they came seeking asylum and refuge from oppression and persecution to safeguard their faith. He recited to the king verses from Surat Marium (Mary, chapter 19) of the Qur'an. The king and his priests were moved because they realized that the words they heard were the truth and were revealed by God. They assured the Muslims that they were safe and could practice their faith without fear.

The Qur'an tells us that it is our obligation to immigrate to a safer place if we fear persecution and oppression.

﴿ إِنَّ ٱلَّذِينَ تَوَفَّىٰهُمُ ٱلْمَلَٰٓئِكَةُ ظَالِمِىٓ أَنفُسِهِمْ قَالُوا۟ فِيمَ كُنتُمْ ۖ قَالُوا۟ كُنَّا مُسْتَضْعَفِينَ فِى ٱلْأَرْضِ
ۚ قَالُوٓا۟ أَلَمْ تَكُنْ أَرْضُ ٱللَّهِ وَٰسِعَةً فَتُهَاجِرُوا۟ فِيهَا ۚ فَأُو۟لَٰٓئِكَ مَأْوَىٰهُمْ جَهَنَّمُ ۖ وَسَآءَتْ مَصِيرًا ﴿٩٧﴾ ﴾

> When the angels take the souls of those who die in sin against their souls, they say: "In what plight were you?" They reply: "Weak and oppressed in the earth we were." They say: "Was not the earth of Allah spacious enough for you to move away?" Such will find their abode in Hell, what an evil refuge. (An-Nisa' [The Women] 4:97)

A just ruler does not pass judgment till he hears both sides of the story in order to ascertain the truth. The king, once he was convinced, allowed the Muslims to practice their religion of Islam with no fear, though he was a Christian. Both Islam and Christianity came from the same source: the one and only God, and both religions preach the truth from God.

The Boycott

The leaders of Quraish were afraid of killing Muhammad because his clan would retaliate and war would occur. They decided instead to boycott Muhammad and his clan. The prophet and his clan were forced to retreat to a narrow passage in the mountains around Macca. They stayed there for three years facing hunger, isolation, and great difficulty.

The boycott had the opposite effect in that others wondered about the cruelty and injustice of the Quraish to their own people. The boycott then ended after three years.

In the tenth year after the revelation, the prophet's wife died. She was a great source of comfort and support to him. Also, his uncle, who stood by him and supported him though he did not accept Islam, died. This year is called the year of mourning.

The prophet and the Muslims faced difficult times, but their faith was strong, and they never lost hope. The Qur'an came down urging patience and perseverance and promising God's help and victory in due time.

﴿ أَمْ حَسِبْتُمْ أَن تَدْخُلُوا۟ ٱلْجَنَّةَ وَلَمَّا يَأْتِكُم مَّثَلُ ٱلَّذِينَ خَلَوْا۟ مِن قَبْلِكُم ۖ مَّسَّتْهُمُ ٱلْبَأْسَآءُ وَٱلضَّرَّآءُ
وَزُلْزِلُوا۟ حَتَّىٰ يَقُولَ ٱلرَّسُولُ وَٱلَّذِينَ ءَامَنُوا۟ مَعَهُۥ مَتَىٰ نَصْرُ ٱللَّهِ ۗ أَلَآ إِنَّ نَصْرَ ٱللَّهِ قَرِيبٌ ﴾

> Did you think that you will enter paradise without such trials as came to those who passed away before you? They encountered suffering and adversity, and

were so shaken in spirit that even the messenger and those of faith with him cried: "When the help of Allah will come?" Indeed the help of Allah is always near! (Al-Baqara [The Cow] 2:214)

The Journey to Ta'if and the Dua'a of the Prophet

The prophet went to Ta'if, about sixty miles from Macca, to invite its leaders to Islam. They ridiculed him and incited the mob to throw stones at him. He complained to God about his weakness and lack of resources, but he would remain steadfast in his mission. What he cared about whether God was upset with him! He did not seek personal revenge from those who harmed him. He wanted them to be guided. God heard his prayer and reassured him that He was not angry with him.

To complain to God and seek His help is a form of worship. On whom do we call if not on God! He knows what difficulty we are experiencing, and He will help us. We should patiently persevere.

﴿ وَإِن يَمْسَسْكَ ٱللَّهُ بِضُرٍّ فَلَا كَاشِفَ لَهُۥٓ إِلَّا هُوَ

If God touch you with affliction, none can remove it but He. (Al-An'am [The Cattle] 6:17)

Isra' and Mir'aj (Night Journey and Ascension to the Heavens)

God wanted to strengthen the heart of Prophet Muhammad (PBUH) and show him the wonders of the heavens, so the angel Gabriel took him on a night journey from the sacred mosque in Macca to the farthest mosque in Jerusalem. Then they ascended to the heavens and met other prophets there. Then he was presented to God, who inspired to him what He willed. The five daily prayers were ordained on Muslims at that time. This journey occurred on the eleventh year after the revelation. The Qur'an confirms that this journey did in fact take place:

﴿ سُبۡحَٰنَ ٱلَّذِيٓ أَسۡرَىٰ بِعَبۡدِهِۦ لَيۡلٗا مِّنَ ٱلۡمَسۡجِدِ ٱلۡحَرَامِ إِلَى ٱلۡمَسۡجِدِ ٱلۡأَقۡصَا ٱلَّذِي بَٰرَكۡنَا
حَوۡلَهُۥ لِنُرِيَهُۥ مِنۡ ءَايَٰتِنَآۚ إِنَّهُۥ هُوَ ٱلسَّمِيعُ ٱلۡبَصِيرُ ١ ﴾

> Glory to God who did take His servant for a journey by night, from the sacred mosque to the farthest mosque, whose precincts We did bless in order to show him Our signs; for He is the one Who hears and sees all things. (Al-Isra' [Night Journey] 17:1)

﴿ مَا كَذَبَ ٱلۡفُؤَادُ مَا رَأَىٰٓ ١١ أَفَتُمَٰرُونَهُۥ عَلَىٰ مَا يَرَىٰ ١٢ وَلَقَدۡ رَءَاهُ نَزۡلَةً أُخۡرَىٰ ١٣ عِندَ
سِدۡرَةِ ٱلۡمُنتَهَىٰ ١٤ عِندَهَا جَنَّةُ ٱلۡمَأۡوَىٰٓ ١٥ إِذۡ يَغۡشَى ٱلسِّدۡرَةَ مَا يَغۡشَىٰ ١٦ مَا زَاغَ ٱلۡبَصَرُ وَمَا
طَغَىٰ ١٧ لَقَدۡ رَأَىٰ مِنۡ ءَايَٰتِ رَبِّهِ ٱلۡكُبۡرَىٰٓ ١٨ ﴾

> The Prophet's heart and mind in no way falsified that which he saw. Will you then dispute with him concerning what he saw? For indeed he saw him at a second descent, near the Lote Tree of the utmost boundary. Near it is the Garden of abode. Behold! The Lote Tree was shrouded with what shrouds. His sight never swerved, nor did it go wrong. For truly did he see, of the signs of his Lord, the greatest. (An-Najm [The Star] 53:11–18)

This night journey was a private showing for Prophet Muhammad (PBUH). It was a miracle witnessed only by the prophet. Some Muslims, on hearing of this journey, did not believe it and turned away from their Islam.

Prophet Muhammad met with other prophets in heaven. They approved of his mission because God took a covenant from them to believe and support His messengers and prophets. Prophet Muhammad (PBUH) came to complete the work of those before him. There will be no messengers after him. Therefore, he was sent to all mankind, not just Muslims.

The journey from Macca to Al-Quds (Jerusalem) illustrates the bond between all religions. Al-Quds is the birthplace of Abraham, Jacob, Moses, and Jesus. Mecca is the birthplace of Muhammad.

Mir'aj or ascension to the heavens coincides with the five daily prayers ordained on Muslims. During prayer, Muslims are close to God and receive His guidance and mercy.

Immigration to Madinah

As Prophet Muhammad (PBUH) invited people to Islam during the hajj (pilgrimage), a group from Madinah listened to him and accepted Islam. The next year, twelve men came and gave their pledge to the prophet to obey him. One of the prophet's companions went to Madinah to teach the new Muslims their religion and recite the Qur'an. Islam spread rapidly in Madina. The next year, the thirteenth year after the revelation, seventy-three men and two women gave their pledge at Aqaba. This pledge was to hear and obey, in God's cause, to enjoin good and forbid evil, not to be afraid of blame when serving God, and to defend and support the prophet when he comes to Madinah.

It is the wisdom of God that Islam would take hold in Madinah after the difficulties Muslims encountered in Macca. It was the effort of Mosa'b, the prophet's companion, that Islam spread widely in Madinah.

The duty of Muslims is to hear God's message and obey the messenger of God.

وَقَالُوا۟ سَمِعْنَا وَأَطَعْنَا ۖ غُفْرَانَكَ رَبَّنَا وَإِلَيْكَ ٱلْمَصِيرُ

And they say: "We hear and we obey. We seek Your forgiveness our Lord, to You is the end of all journeys." (Al-Baqara [The Cow] 2:285)

Since Islam now had a base in Madinah, the prophet ordered the Muslims to immigrate to Yathrib, now called Madinah (the city of the prophet).

Muhammad and Abu Bakr Journey from Macca to Madinah

Abu Bakr was Muhammad's trusted advisor and intimate friend. He accompanied him during the journey from Macca to Madinah. They hid in a cave for a few days to throw off the Quraish chasing them. The prophet first arrived in Qoba'a and built the mosque there. Then he entered Madinah, where the Muslims were waiting for him and were very happy to see him for the first time.

When our *da'wa* fails in one place, it is time to move to another place. Macca resisted the prophet, and despite his effort there for thirteen years, few accepted Islam. Since Islam found a new home in Madinah, it was the responsibility of Muslims to immigrate to Madinah and help their brothers establish and defend the Muslim state. If anyone does not do that, then he is negligent in his duty.

﴿ وَمَن يُشَاقِقِ ٱلرَّسُولَ مِنۢ بَعۡدِ مَا تَبَيَّنَ لَهُ ٱلۡهُدَىٰ وَيَتَّبِعۡ غَيۡرَ سَبِيلِ ٱلۡمُؤۡمِنِينَ نُوَلِّهِۦ مَا تَوَلَّىٰ
وَنُصۡلِهِۦ جَهَنَّمَۖ وَسَآءَتۡ مَصِيرًا ١١٥ ﴾

> If anyone contends with the messenger, after guidance has been conveyed to him, and follows a path other than that of men of faith, We shall leave

him in the path he has chosen, and land him in hell, what an evil refuge. (An-Nisa' [The Women] 4:115)

The Muslims in Madinah were very happy to see the prophet. This joy and happiness is a natural feeling in the hearts of Muslims toward God's prophet. He represented God's blessings and mercy, and he taught Muslims their faith and religion. He symbolized Islam. More than fourteen centuries have passed, yet the love for the prophet still fills the hearts of millions of Muslims all over the world. Loving the prophet implies obeying his orders and following his example.

The Problems the Prophet Faced in Madinah and How He Solved Them

Prophet Muhammad (PBUH) faced many problems in Madinah. We will discuss some of these problems and the prophet's approach of solving them.

1. There were different groups in Madinah with diverse interests. The residents in Madinah, called Ansar (allies), were of two main tribes. They used to fight each other and were enemies for many years. There was an influx of immigrants (*muhajirun*) from Mecca. They were poor as their possessions were left back home or confiscated by Quraish.

2. There were three Jewish tribes in Madinah. They had control over the economy and did not welcome the new Muslim influence.
3. Many residents in Madinah were hypocrites. They confessed faith, but their hearts did not submit. They waited to see who had the upper hand to join the victor.
4. The economic situation in Madinah was poor and getting worse because of the influx of refugees.
5. The *kuffar* (Unbelievers) of the Quraish were waiting to fight and destroy the Muslim state in Madinah.
6. Calling to God must continue, and the education of the Muslims on their faith is an ongoing process.

The Prophet's (PBUH) Plan

Establishing the mosque as the focal point in the lives of Muslims.

They worshiped there every day together. They met and began to know one another. They helped one another and worked together. The mosque also served as a shelter for poor Muslims who had no other place to stay.

The Qur'an praises a mosque in Madinah that was established on righteousness.

لَّمَسْجِدٌ أُسِّسَ عَلَى ٱلتَّقْوَىٰ مِنْ أَوَّلِ يَوْمٍ أَحَقُّ أَن تَقُومَ فِيهِ

> There is a mosque whose foundation was laid from the first day on piety; it is more worthy of your standing therein. (At-Tawbah [Repentance] 9:108)

The behavior of those frequenting the mosque and are devoted to God is described in the Qur'an:

﴿ فِي بُيُوتٍ أَذِنَ ٱللَّهُ أَن تُرۡفَعَ وَيُذۡكَرَ فِيهَا ٱسۡمُهُۥ يُسَبِّحُ لَهُۥ فِيهَا بِٱلۡغُدُوِّ وَٱلۡأٓصَالِ ۝ رِجَالٞ
لَّا تُلۡهِيهِمۡ تِجَٰرَةٞ وَلَا بَيۡعٌ عَن ذِكۡرِ ٱللَّهِ وَإِقَامِ ٱلصَّلَوٰةِ وَإِيتَآءِ ٱلزَّكَوٰةِ يَخَافُونَ يَوۡمٗا تَتَقَلَّبُ فِيهِ
ٱلۡقُلُوبُ وَٱلۡأَبۡصَٰرُ ۝ ﴾

> In houses, which God has permitted to be raised, to honor and celebrate His name and He is glorified by morning and evening, by men whom neither trade nor sale can divert them from the remembrance of God, nor from regular prayer, nor from giving charity; their fear is the Day when hearts and eyes will be turned about. (An-Nur [The Light] 24:36–37)

Establishing a covenant of brotherhood between the immigrants and the allies.

This way, each member of the Ansar (allies) would take a member of the *muhajirun* (immigrants) as a brother to support him and help him till he is able to stand on his own. The Ansars opened their homes and their hearts to their immigrant brothers and shared with them whatever they had willingly. Such friendship and love worked because

God allowed and nurtured this feeling of belonging, unity, love, and friendship.

هُوَ ٱلَّذِىٓ أَيَّدَكَ بِنَصْرِهِۦ وَبِٱلْمُؤْمِنِينَ ﴿٦٢﴾ وَأَلَّفَ بَيْنَ قُلُوبِهِمْ ۚ لَوْ أَنفَقْتَ مَا فِى ٱلْأَرْضِ
جَمِيعًا مَّآ أَلَّفْتَ بَيْنَ قُلُوبِهِمْ وَلَٰكِنَّ ٱللَّهَ أَلَّفَ بَيْنَهُمْ ۚ إِنَّهُۥ عَزِيزٌ حَكِيمٌ ﴿٦٣﴾ ﴾

> Allah strengthened you with His aid and with the believers; and He put affection in their hearts. If you spent all that is on earth, you could not have produced this affection, but Allah has done it, for He is exalted in might, wise. (Al-Anfal [Spoils of War] 8:62–63)

The Qur'an praised both the immigrants, who left their homes to support God's messenger, and the allies, who gave them shelter and support.

﴿ لِلْفُقَرَآءِ ٱلْمُهَٰجِرِينَ ٱلَّذِينَ أُخْرِجُوا۟ مِن دِيَٰرِهِمْ وَأَمْوَٰلِهِمْ يَبْتَغُونَ فَضْلًا مِّنَ ٱللَّهِ وَرِضْوَٰنًا
وَيَنصُرُونَ ٱللَّهَ وَرَسُولَهُۥٓ ۚ أُو۟لَٰٓئِكَ هُمُ ٱلصَّٰدِقُونَ ﴿٨﴾ وَٱلَّذِينَ تَبَوَّءُو ٱلدَّارَ وَٱلْإِيمَٰنَ مِن قَبْلِهِمْ
يُحِبُّونَ مَنْ هَاجَرَ إِلَيْهِمْ وَلَا يَجِدُونَ فِى صُدُورِهِمْ حَاجَةً مِّمَّآ أُوتُوا۟ وَيُؤْثِرُونَ عَلَىٰٓ أَنفُسِهِمْ وَلَوْ
كَانَ بِهِمْ خَصَاصَةٌ ۚ وَمَن يُوقَ شُحَّ نَفْسِهِۦ فَأُو۟لَٰٓئِكَ هُمُ ٱلْمُفْلِحُونَ ﴿٩﴾ ﴾

> To the indigent Muhajirs, those who were expelled from their homes and their property while seeking grace from Allah and his good pleasure, and aiding Allah and His messenger, such are indeed the truthful. And those who before them had homes in Medina, and had adopted the faith; show their

> affection to such as came to them for refuge, and entertain no desire in their hearts for things given to the Muhajirs, but give them preference over themselves, even though they were poor; those saved from the covetousness of their own souls will achieve prosperity. (Al-Hashr [The Gathering] 59:8–9)

This bond of brotherhood served many useful purposes:

- It gave relief to the economy of Madinah as it shifted the burden of aiding the refugees from the state to individual members of society.
- It dissolved many of the causes of division between Muslims, such as tribal loyalty, race, and wealth. A nobleman became a brother to a slave. The Muslims were taught that before God they are all equal, except for piety.
- It taught the Muslims that they can certainly work together.
- It provided a sense of belonging and identity.
- It also provided a stimulus to protect the Muslim community.

The Qur'an stresses that men and women of faith are guardians and protectors of one another, and they share one faith and serve and obey one God.

﴿ وَٱلْمُؤْمِنُونَ وَٱلْمُؤْمِنَٰتُ بَعْضُهُمْ أَوْلِيَآءُ بَعْضٍۚ يَأْمُرُونَ بِٱلْمَعْرُوفِ وَيَنْهَوْنَ عَنِ ٱلْمُنكَرِ
وَيُقِيمُونَ ٱلصَّلَوٰةَ وَيُؤْتُونَ ٱلزَّكَوٰةَ وَيُطِيعُونَ ٱللَّهَ وَرَسُولَهُۥٓۚ أُوْلَٰٓئِكَ سَيَرْحَمُهُمُ ٱللَّهُۗ إِنَّ ٱللَّهَ
عَزِيزٌ حَكِيمٌ ٧١ ﴾

> The believers, men and women, are protectors one of another: they enjoin what is just, and forbid what is evil; they observe regular prayers, and give in charity, and obey God and His messenger; on them God will pour His mercy; for God is exalted in power, wise. (At-Tawbah [Repentance] 9:71)

Establishing a covenant of nonaggression and cooperation between the Muslims and the Jewish tribes.

In this treaty, the lives, properties, and possessions of the Jews were protected. They were free to practice their religion and were not forced to accept Islam. If a Jew is wronged, the state would ensure justice for him, as it would for a Muslim. In return the Jews were asked to help and support the Muslim state and defend it against their enemies.

Initially the Jews appeared to accept the terms of this treaty but soon afterward began to work with the hypocrites in Madinah and with the *kuffar* of Quraish to undermine the Muslim state. They knew that the time had come for a new prophet to appear. They had hoped that he would be a Jew, like other prophets before. When Prophet Muhammad (PBUH) came confirming the teachings of previous prophets, the Jews rejected him because he was an Arab, and they despised the Arabs. The Qur'an documents their feelings:

ذَٰلِكَ بِأَنَّهُمْ قَالُوا۟ لَيْسَ عَلَيْنَا فِى ٱلْأُمِّيِّـۧنَ سَبِيلٌ

> Because they say: "No blame can attach to us for anything that we may do with regards to the unlettered people." (Al-Imran [The Family of Imran] 3:75)

They knew Muhammad to be God's prophet and messenger, but they denied him and refused to accept him as God's prophet.

﴿ وَلَمَّا جَآءَهُمْ رَسُولٌ مِّنْ عِندِ ٱللَّهِ مُصَدِّقٌ لِّمَا مَعَهُمْ نَبَذَ فَرِيقٌ مِّنَ ٱلَّذِينَ أُوتُوا۟ ٱلْكِتَٰبَ كِتَٰبَ ٱللَّهِ وَرَآءَ ظُهُورِهِمْ كَأَنَّهُمْ لَا يَعْلَمُونَ ﴿١٠١﴾ ﴾

> When there came to them a messenger from God, confirming what was with them, a party of the people of the Book threw away the Book of God as if they did not know. (Al-Baqara [The Cow] 2:101)

The Jews in Madinah tried to distort the truth and make people doubt the authenticity of the Qur'an. They worked with the hypocrites to cause division among the Muslims. They also collaborated with the enemies of the Muslim state.

Protecting the Muslim state against its enemies.

The prophet (PBUH) ordered the Muslims to be ready and prepare themselves to defend their city against attacks. The Qur'an orders Muslims to be strong in order to repel possible attacks. Their enemies waited for any sign of weakness.

﴿ وَأَعِدُّوا لَهُم مَّا ٱسْتَطَعْتُم مِّن قُوَّةٍ وَمِن رِّبَاطِ ٱلْخَيْلِ تُرْهِبُونَ بِهِۦ عَدُوَّ ٱللَّهِ وَعَدُوَّكُمْ
وَءَاخَرِينَ مِن دُونِهِمْ لَا تَعْلَمُونَهُمُ ٱللَّهُ يَعْلَمُهُمْ ﴾

> Therefore, make ready against them whatever force and war mounts you are able to muster, so that you might deter the enemies of God who are your enemies as well, and others besides them of whom you are unaware, but God knows them. (Al-Anfal [Spoils of War] 8:60)

Educating the Muslims and preparing them to carry on the work of da'wa.

Despite all the difficulties the Muslims had encountered, it was necessary to continue spreading Islam and inviting people to God by wisdom and good example. Therefore, the prophet spent a lot of time educating and grooming a group of young people to carry on the work of da'wa. They followed the example of their teacher in applying the

Qur'an, understanding morals and ethics, talking to people, and letting them understand the teachings of Islam.

The prophet taught them to do the following:

- Love for your brother as you love for yourself.
- A Muslim is he with whom other Muslims feel safe and do not fear harm from his tongue or his hand.
- Spread greetings of peace, provide food for the needy, keep close to your relations, and pray at night while others sleep. Then will you enter heaven in peace.
- The Muslim is the brother of another Muslim. He does not wrong him nor fails him nor leaves him to his enemy. Whoever is helping his brother, Allah will help him. Whoever relieves the difficulty of a Muslim, Allah will relieve his difficulty on the Day of Judgment. Whoever shields and protects a Muslim, Allah will shield him and protect him on the Day of Judgment.
- The Qur'an orders Muslims to invite others to Islam with conviction and clear insight:

﴿ قُلْ هَٰذِهِۦ سَبِيلِىٓ أَدْعُوٓا۟ إِلَى ٱللَّهِ ۚ عَلَىٰ بَصِيرَةٍ أَنَا۠ وَمَنِ ٱتَّبَعَنِى

Say: "This is my way, I do invite to Allah with conviction and clear insight, I and those who follow me." (Youseff [Joseph] 12:108)

Those doing da'wa must understand clearly the message of Islam, be knowledgeable and wise, show that they care, and set a good example in their character and behavior.

﴿ ٱدْعُ إِلَىٰ سَبِيلِ رَبِّكَ بِٱلْحِكْمَةِ وَٱلْمَوْعِظَةِ ٱلْحَسَنَةِ ۖ وَجَٰدِلْهُم بِٱلَّتِى هِىَ أَحْسَنُ ۚ

> Invite to the way of your Lord with wisdom and good example, and argue with them only in ways that are best. (An-Nahl [The Bees] 16:125)

The Prophet's Character

Prophet Muhammad (PBUH) was successful because of his morals and noble character. How he approached and solved the problems in Madinah is evidence of his wisdom and sound judgment. He was eloquent and able to communicate. He used clear short sentences and repeated his sayings so that those listening to him can understand and remember his instructions. For example, he said, "Fear God at all times; follow a bad deed with a good deed, it will wipe out; and interact with people on the basis of morals and noble character." He also said, "A strong person is not the one who is strong physically, but he is the one who can control his anger."

He was kind, gentle, and caring. The Qur'an describes this character of the prophet:

﴿ فَبِمَا رَحْمَةٍ مِّنَ ٱللَّهِ لِنتَ لَهُمْ ۖ وَلَوْ كُنتَ فَظًّا غَلِيظَ ٱلْقَلْبِ لَٱنفَضُّوا۟ مِنْ حَوْلِكَ ۖ فَٱعْفُ عَنْهُمْ
وَٱسْتَغْفِرْ لَهُمْ وَشَاوِرْهُمْ فِى ٱلْأَمْرِ

> It was Allah's mercy and grace that you dealt with them gently; if you were sever or harsh-hearted, they would have broken away from you. Therefore pardon them and seek forgiveness for them, and consult them in your mutual affairs. (Al-Imran [The Family of Imran] 3:159)

The prophet was forgiving and tolerant. He truly cared and wanted to guide the way to God. He was truthful and honest. At the same time he was humble and shy. He was generous, especially in the fasting month of Ramadan. He patiently persevered despite the difficulties that he encountered throughout his life. He never lost hope in God's mercy. He was just, even with his enemies. He did not care for the material things in life and preferred God's reward in the hereafter. He was a devout worshipper and spent hours praying at night. The Qur'an states,

﴿ وَلَا تَمُدَّنَّ عَيْنَيْكَ إِلَىٰ مَا مَتَّعْنَا بِهِۦٓ أَزْوَٰجًا مِّنْهُمْ زَهْرَةَ ٱلْحَيَوٰةِ ٱلدُّنْيَا لِنَفْتِنَهُمْ فِيهِ ۚ وَرِزْقُ رَبِّكَ
خَيْرٌ وَأَبْقَىٰ ﴿١٣١﴾ وَأْمُرْ أَهْلَكَ بِٱلصَّلَوٰةِ وَٱصْطَبِرْ عَلَيْهَا ۖ لَا نَسْـَٔلُكَ رِزْقًا ۖ نَّحْنُ نَرْزُقُكَ ۗ وَٱلْعَـٰقِبَةُ لِلتَّقْوَىٰ
﴿١٣٢﴾ ﴾

> Do not strain your eyes in longing for the things We have given for enjoyment to parties of them, the

splendor of the life of this world, through which We test them; but the provision of your Lord is better, and more enduring. Enjoin prayer on your people, and be constant therein. We ask you not to provide sustenance. We provide it for you. But the Hereafter is for the righteous. (Taha 20:131–132)

The Qur'an confirms the noble character of the prophet:

﴿ وَإِنَّكَ لَعَلَىٰ خُلُقٍ عَظِيمٍ ﴿٤﴾ ﴾

You are indeed on an exalted standard of character. (Al-Qalam [The Pen] 68:4)

Fasting the Month of Ramadan

In the second year after Hijra (immigration) to Medina, the order came from God that Muslims must fast the month of Ramadan. Ramadan is the ninth lunar month in the Muslim calendar. It is the month when the revelation of the Qur'an began. Muslims fast from dawn till sunset and abstain from food, drink, and desires. The fast is intended to learn self-restraint, patience, and commitment and to get close to God and acknowledge his blessings. During Ramadan, Muslims safeguard their prayers and offer additional prayers, especially in congregation at night. They read the Qur'an and give to charity. Ramadan is a blessed month with many rewards. The Qur'an states,

﴿ يَٰٓأَيُّهَا ٱلَّذِينَ ءَامَنُوا۟ كُتِبَ عَلَيْكُمُ ٱلصِّيَامُ كَمَا كُتِبَ عَلَى ٱلَّذِينَ مِن قَبْلِكُمْ لَعَلَّكُمْ تَتَّقُونَ ﴿١٨٣﴾ ﴾

> O you who believe fasting has been ordained on you, as it was ordained on those before you, that you may learn Taqwa (self-restraint). (Al-Baqara [The Cow] 2:183)

﴿ شَهْرُ رَمَضَانَ ٱلَّذِىٓ أُنزِلَ فِيهِ ٱلْقُرْءَانُ هُدًى لِّلنَّاسِ وَبَيِّنَٰتٍ مِّنَ ٱلْهُدَىٰ وَٱلْفُرْقَانِ

> Ramadan is the month in which the Qur'an was sent down, as a guide to mankind, also clear signs for guidance and judgment between right and wrong. (Al-Baqara [The Cow] 2:185)

God gives the reward of the fast. Prophet Muhammad (PBUH) related after his Lord,

> Fasting is done for My sake, and I give its reward. Fasting is protection. When one is fasting, he should not use bad language or raise his voice. If someone curses him or picks a fight with him, he should say: "I am fasting". He leaves his food, and drink and desires for My sake. A fasting person has two joys: once when he breaks his fast, he is happy that he can eat; and when he meets his lord, he is happy that he fasted. (Narrated by Bukhari)

The Prohibition of Alcohol

The order to prohibit alcohol on Muslims passed through several stages. First they were told that there is some benefit but a lot of harm in alcohol. Next they were warned not to pray when intoxicated; otherwise, they can say wrong things. Then the final prohibition came later.

﴿ يَٰٓأَيُّهَا ٱلَّذِينَ ءَامَنُوٓا۟ إِنَّمَا ٱلْخَمْرُ وَٱلْمَيْسِرُ وَٱلْأَنصَابُ وَٱلْأَزْلَٰمُ رِجْسٌ مِّنْ عَمَلِ ٱلشَّيْطَٰنِ
فَٱجْتَنِبُوهُ لَعَلَّكُمْ تُفْلِحُونَ ﴿٩٠﴾ إِنَّمَا يُرِيدُ ٱلشَّيْطَٰنُ أَن يُوقِعَ بَيْنَكُمُ ٱلْعَدَٰوَةَ وَٱلْبَغْضَآءَ فِى ٱلْخَمْرِ
وَٱلْمَيْسِرِ وَيَصُدَّكُمْ عَن ذِكْرِ ٱللَّهِ وَعَنِ ٱلصَّلَوٰةِ ۖ فَهَلْ أَنتُم مُّنتَهُونَ ﴿٩١﴾ ﴾

> O you who believe intoxicants, gambling, sacrificing to stones and divining the future are evil and the doing of Satan. Then avoid such practices that you may succeed. Satan's plan is to excite enmity and hatred between you with intoxicants and gambling, and hinder you from the remembrance of Allah and from your prayers; will you not then abstain? (Al-Maidah [The Table] 5:90–91)

Alcohol is forbidden in Islam because it clouds the mind and impairs judgment and may lead to other sins.

Fighting in Islam

The Muslims in Mecca were weak and oppressed. They were forced to leave their homes and possessions, and they did immigrate to Medina. The Qur'an documents this injustice:

﴿ ٱلَّذِينَ أُخۡرِجُواْ مِن دِيَٰرِهِم بِغَيۡرِ حَقٍّ إِلَّآ أَن يَقُولُواْ رَبُّنَا ٱللَّهُۗ

> Those who have been driven from their homeland against all right for no reason other than saying: "Our Lord is Allah." (Al-Hajj [Pilgrimage] 22:40)

When the Muslims established their Muslim state in Medina, it was important to prepare themselves in order to defend their city from attacks by their enemies. Permission to fight was then given by God.

﴿ أُذِنَ لِلَّذِينَ يُقَٰتَلُونَ بِأَنَّهُمۡ ظُلِمُواْۚ وَإِنَّ ٱللَّهَ عَلَىٰ نَصۡرِهِمۡ لَقَدِيرٌ ٣٩ ﴾

> Permission (to fight) is given to those against whom war is wrong-fully waged, and indeed Allah has the power to aid them. (Al-Hajj [Pilgrimage] 22:39)

However, fighting in Islam has guidelines that must be followed:

1. Fighting is not done for personal reasons. It is only allowed in the way of God.
2. Fighting is to defend one's country from aggression, not to conquer land.
3. No transgression is allowed.
4. Offers of peace must be accepted.

The Qur'an clearly states that Muslims only fight to defend themselves and only in the cause of God, not for personal reasons. They should not transgress.

﴿ وَقَٰتِلُواْ فِي سَبِيلِ ٱللَّهِ ٱلَّذِينَ يُقَٰتِلُونَكُمۡ وَلَا تَعۡتَدُوٓاْۚ إِنَّ ٱللَّهَ لَا يُحِبُّ ٱلۡمُعۡتَدِينَ ١٩٠ ﴾

> Fight in the cause of Allah those who fight you, but do not commit aggression, for Allah loves not aggressors. (Al-Baqara [The Cow] 2:190)

Prophet Muhammad (PBUH) was asked, "A man fights for gain, and a man fights for fame. Who is fighting in the cause of Allah?" He said, "Only those who fight to make the word of Allah supreme" (narrated by Bukhari). The prophet's battles were to defend the Muslims from their enemies.

There are ethics in fighting. Muslims only fight those engaged in the fighting, not innocent bystanders. The prophet's advice to his troops was, "Do not kill a child, a woman, an elderly person, or anyone not connected with the fighting. Do not burn crops or destroy the land." Captives of war must be treated with human dignity. The dead of the Muslims and their enemies must be buried. Offers of peace must be accepted. The Qur'an states,

﴿ ۞وَإِن جَنَحُواْ لِلسَّلۡمِ فَٱجۡنَحۡ لَهَا وَتَوَكَّلۡ عَلَى ٱللَّهِۚ إِنَّهُۥ هُوَ ٱلسَّمِيعُ ٱلۡعَلِيمُ ٦١ ﴾

> But if they incline to peace, you too should incline to peace, and put your trust in Allah; for he is all-hearing, all-knowing. (Al-Anfal [Spoils of War] 8:61)

Some Muslims claim holy jihad. The Qur'an never mentions the words *holy jihad*. True jihad (striving or fighting) is in the cause of Allah alone. It cannot be invoked by anyone just because he wishes to do so. It can only be invoked by a leader or scholar when a Muslim country is under attack and Muslims must rise to defend themselves from injustice. Holy war is a Christian concept, not a Muslim word.

The Battle of Badr

This occurred in Ramadan on the second year after Hijra. The Muslims left Medina to capture the rich caravan of the Quraish and regain some of the losses they suffered when the Quraish confiscated their possessions. But God had other plans. He wanted the Muslims to fight the *kuffar* (the unbelievers from the Quraish) and defeat them.

The Muslims accomplished a great victory against an army three times their size and better equipped. The Muslims fought with courage and conviction, and that is why they defeated their enemy. However, mistakes were made, and the Qur'an came down to correct these mistakes. They were not fighting for monetary gain but to establish the truth. Therefore, quarreling about the booty was not appropriate. Also, accepting ransom for war criminals was criticized in the Qur'an.

The Battle of Uhud

A large army from Quraish came to Medina to fight and destroy the Muslim state in revenge for their loss at Badr. The hypocrites in Medina retreated with one-third of the army at a critical time, hoping to weaken the resolve of the Muslim fighters.

The archers disobeyed the prophet's orders not to leave their posts and went for the booty. The Quraish attacked the exposed rear of the Muslim army, and the Muslims were confused. Some ran away. They were defeated that day, but the prophet stood his ground. This prevented total disaster, and Muhammad was not killed.

Many valuable lessons are learned from Uhud. God tests his servants sometimes with defeat and sometimes with victory. We need to patiently persevere and not lose heart. The Qur'an states,

﴿ إِن يَمْسَسْكُمْ قَرْحٌ فَقَدْ مَسَّ ٱلْقَوْمَ قَرْحٌ مِّثْلُهُۥ ۚ وَتِلْكَ ٱلْأَيَّامُ نُدَاوِلُهَا بَيْنَ ٱلنَّاسِ وَلِيَعْلَمَ ٱللَّهُ
ٱلَّذِينَ ءَامَنُوا۟ وَيَتَّخِذَ مِنكُمْ شُهَدَآءَ ۗ وَٱللَّهُ لَا يُحِبُّ ٱلظَّٰلِمِينَ ﴿١٤٠﴾ ﴾

> If a wound has touched you, be sure a similar wound has touched the others. Such days of varying fortunes We give to men by turns, that God may know those who believe and that He may take to Himself from your ranks martyrs, for God loves not the wrongdoers. (Al-Imran [The Family of Imran] 3:140)

The Qur'an warned Muslims about the *harmful* effect of the hypocrites and their bad intentions:

﴿ لَوْ خَرَجُوا۟ فِيكُم مَّا زَادُوكُمْ إِلَّا خَبَالًا وَلَأَوْضَعُوا۟ خِلَٰلَكُمْ يَبْغُونَكُمُ ٱلْفِتْنَةَ وَفِيكُمْ سَمَّٰعُونَ لَهُمْ ۗ وَٱللَّهُ عَلِيمٌۢ بِٱلظَّٰلِمِينَ ﴿٤٧﴾ ﴾

> If they go out with you, they would not have increased your strength; rather, they would have caused division and disorder sowing sedition among you, and there would have been among you those who would have listened to them, but Allah knows well the wrong-doers. (At-Tawbah [Repentance] 9:47)

Disobeying the prophet's orders resulted to disaster in Uhud, as it did at other times. The Qur'an reminds us to obey the prophet; otherwise, our deeds will fail.

فَلْيَحْذَرِ ٱلَّذِينَ يُخَالِفُونَ عَنْ أَمْرِهِۦٓ أَن تُصِيبَهُمْ فِتْنَةٌ أَوْ يُصِيبَهُمْ عَذَابٌ أَلِيمٌ

> Let those who disobey the prophet's orders beware, lest they face a trial or grave punishment from Allah. (An-Nur [The Light] 24:63)

The Jews Break Their Covenant and Are Expelled from Madinah

The tribe of Banu Qainuqa broke their covenant and were expelled from Medina. They were allowed to take their possessions with them and were unharmed. The tribe of Bani An-Nadir tried to kill the prophet and declared their hatred to the Muslims. They could no longer be trusted. The Muslims laid siege to their fortifications, and they surrendered. They were also allowed to leave unharmed with their possessions.

The Jews in Madinah were safe, and their rights were protected as long as they lived in peace with the Muslims. But they plotted against the Muslims and broke their covenant. They could no longer be trusted; therefore, they were expelled from Madinah.

The Battle of Ahzab (Confederates)

This occurred in the fifth year after Hijra, when ten thousand fighters marched toward Medina from several Arab tribes, encouraged by the Jewish promise of support. The Muslims dug a trench to prevent their enemies from entering their city. The kuffar laid siege to Medina. Allah sent a windstorm that blew their tents and utensils, and the angels planted fear into the hearts of the confederate forces. They left in a hurry.

﴿ يَٰٓأَيُّهَا ٱلَّذِينَ ءَامَنُوا۟ ٱذْكُرُوا۟ نِعْمَةَ ٱللَّهِ عَلَيْكُمْ إِذْ جَآءَتْكُمْ جُنُودٌ فَأَرْسَلْنَا عَلَيْهِمْ رِيحًا وَجُنُودًا لَّمْ تَرَوْهَا ۚ وَكَانَ ٱللَّهُ بِمَا تَعْمَلُونَ بَصِيرًا ﴾

> O you who believe remember the grace of Allah that He bestowed on you, when there came down on you hosts to overwhelm you. But We sent against them

a hurricane and forces that you did not see; but Allah sees clearly all that you do. (Al-Ahzab [The Confederates] 33:9)

Banu Quraiza, who betrayed the Muslims and invited the confederates to lay siege to Medina, surrendered after the Muslims laid siege to their fortresses. They were punished for their treachery.

The Slander Incident

Rumors spread in Medina accusing Aisha, the wife of Prophet Muhammad, of wrongdoing. She was sick at the time and unaware of these malicious rumors. The prophet (PBUH) was hurt as his honor was attacked, but all he did was address the people, wondering why some people are saying bad things about his family!

The Qur'an came down after some time, clearing Aisha from any wrongdoing and warning Muslims not to lie, spread rumors, or attack the honor and integrity of innocent people.

﴿ إِذْ تَلَقَّوْنَهُۥ بِأَلْسِنَتِكُمْ وَتَقُولُونَ بِأَفْوَاهِكُم مَّا لَيْسَ لَكُم بِهِۦ عِلْمٌ وَتَحْسَبُونَهُۥ هَيِّنًا وَهُوَ عِندَ
ٱللَّهِ عَظِيمٌ ﴿١٥﴾ وَلَوْلَآ إِذْ سَمِعْتُمُوهُ قُلْتُم مَّا يَكُونُ لَنَآ أَن نَّتَكَلَّمَ بِهَٰذَا سُبْحَٰنَكَ هَٰذَا بُهْتَٰنٌ
عَظِيمٌ ﴿١٦﴾ يَعِظُكُمُ ٱللَّهُ أَن تَعُودُوا۟ لِمِثْلِهِۦٓ أَبَدًا إِن كُنتُم مُّؤْمِنِينَ ﴿١٧﴾ ﴾

You received it on your tongues and you said out of your mouths things which you had no knowledge;

> and you thought it to be a light matter while it was most serious in the sight of God. Why did you not, when you heard it say: "It is not right of us to speak of this: glory to You, this is a most serious slander!" God does admonish you that you may never repeat such conduct if you are true believers. (An-Nur [The Light] 24:15–17)

We learn that malicious rumors can spread in any community and can cause serious harm. We must stand up against these lies, which ruin the lives of innocent people. The Qur'an explains,

﴿ وَٱلَّذِينَ يُؤْذُونَ ٱلْمُؤْمِنِينَ وَٱلْمُؤْمِنَٰتِ بِغَيْرِ مَا ٱكْتَسَبُوا۟ فَقَدِ ٱحْتَمَلُوا۟ بُهْتَٰنًا وَإِثْمًا مُّبِينًا ﴿٥٨﴾ ﴾

> And those who harm and annoy believing men and women undeservedly, bear on themselves a calumny and a glaring sin. (Al-Ahzab [The Confederates] 33:58)

Though the prophet and his wife were harmed, he patiently waited till God revealed in the Qur'an the innocence of his wife. He did *not* suppress or jail those spreading the rumors because freedom of speech must be guaranteed. Only after their guilt was established were the hypocrites punished.

The Truce of Hudaybiyyah

The Muslims wanted to perform Umrah and Hajj (pilgrimage) to Macca but were prevented by the Quraish. After negotiations, a truce was signed in which the Muslims would be allowed to do the pilgrimage next year, and no fighting would occur for ten years.

This period of peace allowed the Muslims to concentrate their efforts on da'wa, and many people, after hearing the Qur'an, accepted Islam. This truce was a great victory, as the Qur'an explains:

﴿ إِذَا جَآءَ نَصْرُ ٱللَّهِ وَٱلْفَتْحُ ۝ وَرَأَيْتَ ٱلنَّاسَ يَدْخُلُونَ فِى دِينِ ٱللَّهِ أَفْوَاجًا ۝ فَسَبِّحْ بِحَمْدِ رَبِّكَ وَٱسْتَغْفِرْهُ ۚ إِنَّهُۥ كَانَ تَوَّابًۢا ۝ ﴾

> When the help of Allah and victory comes; and you see the people enter the religion of Allah in crowds; celebrate the praises of your Lord, and pray for His forgiveness, for He is often-returning in forgiveness. (An-Nasr [Help] 110:1–3)

The Battle of Khaybar

Khaybar was the headquarters of every enemy of Islam, including the Jews who left Madinah. They collaborated with the enemies of the Muslim state. The Muslim army defeated them and opened their fortresses, and they were allowed to leave for Syria or stay as tenants to farm the land. Their land now belonged to the Muslims.

Prophet Muhammad's Letter to Heads of States, Inviting Them to Islam

Some accepted like the king of Habesha while others refused. In his letter he invited them to worship the one and only God Allah and to believe in him as God's messenger. The Qur'an explains,

﴿ قُلْ يَٰٓأَهْلَ ٱلْكِتَٰبِ تَعَالَوْا۟ إِلَىٰ كَلِمَةٍ سَوَآءٍۭ بَيْنَنَا وَبَيْنَكُمْ أَلَّا نَعْبُدَ إِلَّا ٱللَّهَ وَلَا نُشْرِكَ بِهِۦ شَيْـًٔا
وَلَا يَتَّخِذَ بَعْضُنَا بَعْضًا أَرْبَابًا مِّن دُونِ ٱللَّهِ ۚ فَإِن تَوَلَّوْا۟ فَقُولُوا۟ ٱشْهَدُوا۟ بِأَنَّا مُسْلِمُونَ ﴿٦٤﴾ ﴾

> Say: "O people of the Book, come to a word that is just between us and you, that you worship none but Allah, and that we associate no partners with Him, and that none of us shall take others as lords besides Allah." Then if they turn away, say: "Bear witness that we are Muslims." (Al-Imran [The Family of Imran] 3:64)

The Opening of Mecca

This occurred in the eighth year after Hijra. The Quraish broke their covenant, and the Muslim army marched toward Mecca. The Quraish did not fight, and the prophet entered Macca mounted on his camel, lowering his head out of humility to Allah, not as a conquering worrier. He forgave the same people who forced him out from his birthplace and abused the Muslims, repeating the words of Prophet Youseff (Joseph) when he forgave his brothers.

﴿ قَالَ لَا تَثْرِيبَ عَلَيْكُمُ ٱلْيَوْمَ ۖ يَغْفِرُ ٱللَّهُ لَكُمْ ۖ وَهُوَ أَرْحَمُ ٱلرَّٰحِمِينَ ﴿٩٢﴾ ﴾

> No reproach or blame on you this day; may Allah forgive you, for He is the most merciful of merciful. (Youseff [Joseph] 12:92)

The Quraish were expecting punishment for their crimes, but the prophet forgave them and said, "Go. You are free." The prophet entered the Ka'Ba and destroyed the statues there used as a shrine for idols. The Ka'Ba returned as a symbol of worship and devotion to Allah.

The Delegation from Najran

A Christian delegation from Najran came to Madinah to ask the prophet questions about Eisa (Jesus) and how he was regarded in Islam. When they came wearing silk clothes and gold rings and were arrogant, Muhammad did not return their greetings. When they wore simple clothes and became humble, he greeted them warmly, answered their questions, and allowed them to pray in his mosque according to their tradition.

He made a peace treaty with them in which they governed themselves and kept their faith and paid a tax for protection.

The prophet (PBUH) allowed the Christians to pray in his mosque according to their tradition. He did not force Islam on any of them. We should follow his example and respect the right of others to their faith and convictions.

The Battle of Tabuk

The Muslims left Madinah in the ninth year after Hijra to face the Roman army in order to defend their Muslim state and the Muslims in Syria. The journey was long, and the weather was hot. Food and water were scarce. The weak in faith and the hypocrites preferred their safety and the comfort of their homes.

﴿ فَرِحَ ٱلْمُخَلَّفُونَ بِمَقْعَدِهِمْ خِلَٰفَ رَسُولِ ٱللَّهِ وَكَرِهُوٓا۟ أَن يُجَٰهِدُوا۟ بِأَمْوَٰلِهِمْ وَأَنفُسِهِمْ فِى
سَبِيلِ ٱللَّهِ وَقَالُوا۟ لَا تَنفِرُوا۟ فِى ٱلْحَرِّ ۗ قُلْ نَارُ جَهَنَّمَ أَشَدُّ حَرًّا ۚ لَّوْ كَانُوا۟ يَفْقَهُونَ ﴿٨١﴾ ﴾

> Those who were left behind rejoiced in their sitting back behind the messenger of Allah; they hated to strive and fight, with their goods and persons, in the cause of Allah. They said: "Do not go forth in the heat." Say: "The Fire of Hell is fiercer in heat." If only they could understand. (At-Tawbah [Repentance] 9:81)

Only those Muslims who were true and committed went with the prophet.

﴿ لَٰكِنِ ٱلرَّسُولُ وَٱلَّذِينَ ءَامَنُوا۟ مَعَهُۥ جَٰهَدُوا۟ بِأَمْوَٰلِهِمْ وَأَنفُسِهِمْ ۚ وَأُو۟لَٰٓئِكَ لَهُمُ ٱلْخَيْرَٰتُ ۖ وَأُو۟لَٰٓئِكَ هُمُ ٱلْمُفْلِحُونَ ﴿٨٨﴾ ﴾

> But the messenger and those who believe with him strive and fight with their wealth and their persons; for them are all good things, and it is they who will prosper. (At-Tawbah [Repentance] 9:88)

No fighting occurred since the Romans and their allies retreated deep into Syria. The Arab tribes accepted the rule of Islam. The war with the Romans was in response to the Romans' amazing large army preparing to invade Arabia. It was an act of self-defense.

Coping with difficulty and adversity is what distinguishes those of faith and conviction from those who are weak or are hypocrites.

The Farewell Pilgrimage

Prophet Muhammad (PBUH) did Hajj only once, in the tenth year after Hijra. He showed the Muslims how to perform Hajj, saying, "Take your rites after me and pray as you see me pray."

He circled the Kaaba seven times, which is called *tawaf.* It is a form of prayer, saying *dua'a* (prayer to God) and seeking God's forgiveness. Then he walked between the hills of Safa and Marwah, remembering Hajir, the wife of Ibrahim and the mother of Ismail, when she walked these two hills, searching for water and food for herself and her infant son.

On the ninth day of the month of Zulhijjah (the twelfth month of the lunar calendar), the prophet entered the valley of Arafat, prayed the noon and afternoon prayer together, and stayed there until sunset. The prophet and his companions prayed to God, seeking His forgiveness, mercy, and guidance.

After sunset the prophet went to Muzdalifah, where he prayed the sunset and night prayer together and stayed till dawn. After the dawn prayer he went to Mina.

In Mina he sacrificed the animals and shaved his head. Then he went to Macca to circle the Kaaba then returned to Mina to throw the stones. He repeated this act of throwing the stones two more times as he stayed in Mina for three days.

Muhammad gave a sermon in which he stressed the following:

1. Your souls and possessions are sacred. It is unlawful to kill another human being or to take his possessions.
2. Whoever is trusted, let him give back his trust.

3. Usury is prohibited.
4. You have rights over your wives, and they have rights over you. Fear Allah concerning women.
5. You are going to meet your Lord, and He will ask you about your deeds.
6. I have delivered the message: hold on to the Book of Allah and the Sunnah (tradition) of His prophet, and you will never be misguided.
7. A Muslim is the brother of another Muslim.
8. Allah, have I delivered! The people said, "Yes." Then he said, "O Allah, be a witness."

A Qur'anic verse was revealed in Arafat implying that the message has been completed and that God has accepted Islam as the religion of mankind.

ٱلْيَوْمَ أَكْمَلْتُ لَكُمْ دِينَكُمْ وَأَتْمَمْتُ عَلَيْكُمْ نِعْمَتِى وَرَضِيتُ لَكُمُ ٱلْإِسْلَٰمَ دِينًا

> This day have I perfected your religion for you, completed My favor upon you, and I have chosen for you Islam as your religion. (Al-Maidah [The Table] 5:3)

The Prophet's Last Days

Prophet Muhammad became ill and died in the eleventh year after Hijra. The Qur'an emphasized that Muhammad is *human* and that he would die like other prophets before him.

﴿ إِنَّكَ مَيِّتٌ وَإِنَّهُم مَّيِّتُونَ ﴿٣٠﴾ ﴾

> You are going to die and they are going to die. (Az-Zumar [The Groups] 39:30)

﴿ وَمَا مُحَمَّدٌ إِلَّا رَسُولٌ قَدْ خَلَتْ مِن قَبْلِهِ ٱلرُّسُلُ ﴾

> Muhammad is only a messenger; many messengers passed away before him. (Al-Imran [The Family of Imran] 3:144)

Muslims do not worship Muhammad. Muslims worship Allah alone with no partners.

Before the prophet's death, he asked if he offended anyone or wronged anyone in the least. If he did, he asked the person wronged to exact retribution and forgive him. We should follow his example and seek forgiveness from those whom we may have offended before a day comes when this is too late.

Prophet Muhammad left no money. During his life all his possessions went to the poor and needy. What he left is his Sunnah and his example, a legacy that did not die in his death.

7

The Tradition Sunnah of Prophet Muhammad (PBUH)

The Sunnah and Hadith

The Sunnah includes three things:

1. What the Prophet Muhammad (PBUH) said
2. What the prophet did
3. What he approved of or did not object to concerning the sayings, or actions of his companions in his presence

The Hadith (sayings) is what the prophet said on different occasions. Therefore, the Sunnah is more encompassing than the Hadith.

How the Sunnah Was Preserved

The prophet's sayings were memorized, and some of them were written by his companions and later on compiled in books of the Hadith. Memorization was, however, the predominant method. What helped preserve the Sunnah is the following:

1. The prophet used clear short sentences and repeated his words so that those listening to him could understand and memorize his words.
2. The Arabs at that time were gifted with the ability to memorize. They could listen to a long poem and repeat it word for word.
3. The prophet's companions understood the importance of his sayings and of preserving his Sunnah for future generations. They worked hard to convey what they memorized and were honest. Some of them studied his sayings at night to make sure they delivered it correctly. The prophet (PBUH) said, "May Allah reward the person who hears what I say, memorize it and delivers it accurately, for a person may carry knowledge and he himself is not a scholar, or he may carry knowledge to someone else who has more knowledge" (narrated by Tirmidhi and Ahmad).

4. Allah willed that the Sunnah of His prophet be preserved and allowed the efforts of his companions to succeed.
5. Muslim scholars only accepted the part of the Sunnah that could be authenticated and rejected what could not be proven.

Books of Hadith

These are books that compile the sayings of Prophet Muhammad (PBUH). Some have commentary and explanation. These books can be classified as the following:

1. Authentic Hadith or Sahih (sound), where only what has been highly authenticated and verified is accepted and written
2. Hasan (good), where the sayings are reliable for the most part but less in degree of authenticity
3. Other sayings that may have some weakness

That which was known to be false was rejected and not included. Certain criteria were used to judge the authenticity of the Hadith:

1. The *narrator* of the Hadith was the person who related this Hadith and attributed it to Prophet Muhammad (PBUH). The character of this person

was investigated: Was he an honest righteous person? Could he have lied? His ability to memorize was also questioned: did his memory fail him when he got old?

Also, where did he hear the Hadith and from whom? Did he meet that person? Is there any doubt about this narration because it contradicts another authentic Hadith, the Qur'an, or an established rule in Islam?

2. The series of men who related the prophet's sayings. Each of these men was scrutinized as to their honesty, integrity, and memorization. Did each one truly hear the Hadith from whom he stated he heard it? If each one of these men passed this rigorous test, then this series is called a golden series and is accepted. Bukhari and Muslim only relate the Hadith by a series of men who were exemplary and highly reliable.
3. The content of the Hadith was examined to determine it if it was logical, confirmed the Qur'an, did not contradict another authentic Hadith, and had no apparent weakness.

The important books of the Hadith are Bukhari, Muslim, Malik, Tirmidhi, Abu Dawood, Ahmad, Nesa'ee, Ibn Majah, Hakim. Bukhari and Muslim are the two most authentic books of the Hadith.

The Role of the Sunnah

The Qur'an explains that Prophet Muhammad (PBUH) serves several important functions:

Delivering God's message accurately.

The Prophet delivered what was inspired to him from God without adding or deleting anything from the divine message.

۞ يَـٰٓأَيُّهَا ٱلرَّسُولُ بَلِّغْ مَآ أُنزِلَ إِلَيْكَ مِن رَّبِّكَ ۖ وَإِن لَّمْ تَفْعَلْ فَمَا بَلَّغْتَ رِسَالَتَهُۥ

> O messenger deliver what has been sent down to you from your Lord; If you did not then you would not have delivered His message. (Al-Maidah [The Table] 5:67)

Explaining God's message.

وَأَنزَلْنَآ إِلَيْكَ ٱلذِّكْرَ لِتُبَيِّنَ لِلنَّاسِ مَا نُزِّلَ إِلَيْهِمْ وَلَعَلَّهُمْ يَتَفَكَّرُونَ

> We sent to you the message in order that you may explain to mankind what was sent down to them from their Lord, that they may reflect. (An-Nahl [The Bees] 16:44)

The Qur'an tells Muslims to pray and teaches them the rationale and value of prayer. It was, however, Prophet

Muhammad (PBUH) who explained in detail how to pray and what to say during prayer. He said, "Pray as you see me pray" (narrated by Bukhari). The prophet also explained the details and manner of fasting, charity, pilgrimage, interaction with other Muslims—being good to our neighbors and families and helping those who need our help—and what it means to have faith and serve God. A Muslim cannot live his Islam by the Qur'an alone. He needs the Sunnah, which explains how to apply the guidelines of the Qur'an in his life.

Applying God's message in his character and behavior.

This way, the prophet would be the practical application of the Qur'an. When his wife was asked about the character of God's messenger, she said, "His character was the Qur'an" (narrated by Bukhari).

Serving as an example to follow.

We need both a divine book and a human messenger who serves as a model to follow.

﴿ لَّقَدْ كَانَ لَكُمْ فِي رَسُولِ ٱللَّهِ أُسْوَةٌ حَسَنَةٌ

> You have indeed in the messenger of God a good example to follow. (Al-Ahzab [The Confederates] 33:21)

Teaching the Qur'an and Sunnah.

This way, the message is carried over to future generations and is not lost by the death of Muhammad. Prophet Muhammad (PBUH) said, "The best among you is the person who learns the Qur'an, then teaches it to others" (narrated by Bukhari).

Do We Follow Everything the Prophet Said?

Muhammad had a dual role: He was God's prophet and messenger, and as such, Muslims must obey his orders. He was also a human being living in a certain environment, with likes and dislikes. As a man, we follow the noble character of Muhammad but not necessarily everything that he did.

Some Muslims follow the literal words of the Hadith. This may be appropriate at times but, at other times, inappropriate . For example, the prophet (PBUH) once said, "What is below the ankle is in hellfire." This statement does not mean that Muslims must wear short pants. The prophet saw a man walking arrogantly with his robe washing the floor, so he made this comment to warn us against arrogance and to tell us to be humble. The Qur'an confirms this concept:

﴿ وَلَا تَمْشِ فِي ٱلْأَرْضِ مَرَحًا ۖ إِنَّكَ لَن تَخْرِقَ ٱلْأَرْضَ وَلَن تَبْلُغَ ٱلْجِبَالَ طُولًا ۝٣٧ ﴾

> Nor walk on earth with insolence, for you cannot rend the earth asunder, nor reach the mountains in height. (Al-Isra' [Night Journey] 17:37)

Therefore, we need to understand the prophet's sayings in the context of the Qur'an and to find out if the prophet's words were made for a specific reason that applied to his time or a general order that is applicable at all times. An example of this is the prophet saying, "I have been commanded to fight An-Nas till they bear witness that there is no god except Allah, and that I am His messenger" (narrated by Muslim). Some take the prophet's words literally and understand that the prophet was ordered by God to fight all mankind till they submit in Islam. However, this understanding contradicts the Qur'an because as Muslims we cannot force anyone to become a Muslim. God gave man a free choice: to believe or reject faith. The word *An-Nas* here refers to the tribe of Quraish, not mankind. The prophet was ordered to fight the Quraish because they were enemies.

8

What Does Muhammad Represent to Muslims?

Muslims regard Muhammad as God's prophet and messenger who delivered God's message and, as such, must be obeyed. His Sunnah (tradition) must also be followed because it is an essential part of the religion of Islam. The Qur'an explains the duty of Muslims in obeying God's messenger:

﴿ إِنَّمَا كَانَ قَوْلَ ٱلْمُؤْمِنِينَ إِذَا دُعُوٓاْ إِلَى ٱللَّهِ وَرَسُولِهِۦ لِيَحْكُمَ بَيْنَهُمْ أَن يَقُولُواْ سَمِعْنَا وَأَطَعْنَا
وَأُوْلَٰٓئِكَ هُمُ ٱلْمُفْلِحُونَ ﴿٥١﴾ ﴾

> The answer of the believers, when summoned to Allah and His messenger, in order that he may judge between them, is no other than this: they say: "We hear and we obey'; it is such as these that will succeed. (An-Nur [The Light] 24:51)

To obey the prophet's order is a criterion of faith.

﴿ فَلَا وَرَبِّكَ لَا يُؤْمِنُونَ حَتَّىٰ يُحَكِّمُوكَ فِيمَا شَجَرَ بَيْنَهُمْ ثُمَّ لَا يَجِدُوا فِي أَنفُسِهِمْ حَرَجًا مِّمَّا قَضَيْتَ وَيُسَلِّمُوا تَسْلِيمًا ﴾

> But no, by your Lord, they can have no real faith, until they make you judge in all disputes between them, and find in their souls no resistance against your decisions, but accept them with the fullest conviction. (An-Nisa' [The Women] 4:65)

To obey the prophet is to obey God.

﴿ مَّن يُطِعِ الرَّسُولَ فَقَدْ أَطَاعَ اللَّهَ ﴾

> He who obeys the messenger obeys God. (An-Nisa' [The Women] 4:80)

As we explained before, we need the Sunnah of the prophet in order to apply the teachings of the Qur'an and live our lives as Muslims. Prophet Muhammad (PBUH) stated that he was given the Qur'an and something else similar to it, implying his Sunnah. Therefore, the Sunnah is a divine inspiration, and as such, Muslims should follow and apply the Sunnah.

Muslims also follow the example of Prophet Muhammad (PBUH) in his character and behavior. He applied Qur'anic teachings in his life and became a walking Qur'an, an example to follow. The Qur'an urges Muslims to follow the example of God's messenger:

﴿ لَّقَدْ كَانَ لَكُمْ فِي رَسُولِ ٱللَّهِ أُسْوَةٌ حَسَنَةٌ لِّمَن كَانَ يَرْجُوا ٱللَّهَ وَٱلْيَوْمَ ٱلْآخِرَ وَذَكَرَ ٱللَّهَ كَثِيرًا ﴿٢١﴾ ﴾

> You have in the messenger of God a beautiful example of proper conduct to follow. (Al-Ahzab [The Confederates] 33:21)

He was a father and a husband, and how he treated his family set the pattern for us to follow. He was a friend to his companions and cared for them. He was kind and forgiving. He was a teacher and was effective in relating God's message. He was wise and humble. He was just, even with his enemies. He did not seek personal revenge for himself but made sure that the truth was obvious and needed to be followed. He was devoted to God, the best worshipper. He never gave up hope of God's mercy even in the darkest hour. He put his trust in God and worked hard to accomplish his mission.

Muhammad is human. He was born, and he died, like other messengers before him. The Qur'an emphasizes the human nature of Muhammad in order to make sure that Muslims do not glorify him or worship him.

﴿وَمَا مُحَمَّدٌ إِلَّا رَسُولٌ قَدْ خَلَتْ مِن قَبْلِهِ ٱلرُّسُلُ ۚ أَفَإِي۟ن مَّاتَ أَوْ قُتِلَ ٱنقَلَبْتُمْ عَلَىٰٓ أَعْقَـٰبِكُمْ ۚ وَمَن
يَنقَلِبْ عَلَىٰ عَقِبَيْهِ فَلَن يَضُرَّ ٱللَّهَ شَيْـًٔا ۗ وَسَيَجْزِى ٱللَّهُ ٱلشَّـٰكِرِينَ ﴿١٤٤﴾﴾

> Muhammad is no more than a messenger, many were the messengers that passed away before him. If he died or were killed, will you then turn back on your heels? If any did turn back on his heels, not the least harm will he do to God; but God will reward those who serve Him with gratitude. (Al-Imran [The Family of Imran] 3:144)

Muhammad had no power of his own. He could not benefit or harm on his own. It is God who can help us and benefit us and, if we disobey and punish us.

﴿قُل لَّآ أَمْلِكُ لِنَفْسِى نَفْعًا وَلَا ضَرًّا إِلَّا مَا شَآءَ ٱللَّهُ ۚ وَلَوْ كُنتُ أَعْلَمُ ٱلْغَيْبَ لَٱسْتَكْثَرْتُ مِنَ
ٱلْخَيْرِ وَمَا مَسَّنِىَ ٱلسُّوٓءُ ۚ إِنْ أَنَا۠ إِلَّا نَذِيرٌ وَبَشِيرٌ لِّقَوْمٍ يُؤْمِنُونَ ﴿١٨٨﴾﴾

> Say: "I have no power over any good or harm to myself except as God wills. If I had knowledge of the unseen, I should have multiplied all good, and no evil should have touched me; I am but a warner and a bearer of glad news to those who have faith." (Al-A'raf 7:188)

Muhammad could not guide of his own accord, even to those whom he loved. It is God who guides whom He pleases, and He knows who is ready to receive guidance.

﴿ إِنَّكَ لَا تَهْدِى مَنْ أَحْبَبْتَ وَلَٰكِنَّ ٱللَّهَ يَهْدِى مَن يَشَآءُ ۚ وَهُوَ أَعْلَمُ بِٱلْمُهْتَدِينَ ﴿٥٦﴾ ﴾

> You will not be able to guide everyone whom you love, but God guides whom He will and He knows best those that receive guidance. (Al-Qasas [The Stories] 28:56)

Muslims love Muhammad because he was God's messenger, and they follow his orders and his example as a human being of noble character and morals. He was sent as a mercy to the worlds.

﴿ وَمَآ أَرْسَلْنَٰكَ إِلَّا رَحْمَةً لِّلْعَٰلَمِينَ ﴿١٠٧﴾ ﴾

> We sent you but as a mercy to the worlds. (Al-Anbiya [The Prophets] 21:107)

Muhammad was sent as a universal messenger to all mankind, and he was the last of God's messengers and prophets. There will be no other messenger after him. His message is valid till the Day of Judgment. To conclude, Muslims respect and love Muhammad as God's messenger, but Muslims do not worship Muhammad. Muslims only worship God.

9

Misconceptions About Muhammad

We will discuss the following misconceptions about Muhammad:

1. Muhammad wrote the Qur'an.
2. Muhammad was a man of war.
3. Muhammad married too many wives to satisfy his desires.
4. Muslims worship Muhammad.

Muhammad Wrote the Qur'an

As we discussed before, Muhammad was illiterate: he could not read or write. The Qur'an confirms this fact:

﴿ وَمَا كُنتَ تَتْلُوا۟ مِن قَبْلِهِۦ مِن كِتَٰبٍ وَلَا تَخُطُّهُۥ بِيَمِينِكَ ۖ إِذًا لَّٱرْتَابَ ٱلْمُبْطِلُونَ ﴿٤٨﴾ ﴾

> You were not able to read a book, before this was revealed to you, nor were you able to write it with your right hand, otherwise the talkers of vanity would have doubted (the authenticity of this message). (Al-Ankabut [The Spider] 29:48)

Muhammad was accused, by those who denied that the Qur'an is a divine revelation, of rehearsing tales of the ancient he heard during his travels, and of being taught by others to relate what was dictated to him. The Qur'an relates these accusations then refutes them:

﴿وَقَالُوٓاْ أَسَٰطِيرُ ٱلۡأَوَّلِينَ ٱكۡتَتَبَهَا فَهِيَ تُمۡلَىٰ عَلَيۡهِ بُكۡرَةٗ وَأَصِيلٗا ٥ قُلۡ أَنزَلَهُ ٱلَّذِي يَعۡلَمُ
ٱلسِّرَّ فِي ٱلسَّمَٰوَٰتِ وَٱلۡأَرۡضِۚ إِنَّهُۥ كَانَ غَفُورٗا رَّحِيمٗا ٦﴾

> And they say: "Tales of the ancient, which he caused to be written, and they are dictated to him morning and evening." Say: "The (Qur'an) was sent down by Him who knows the secret in the heavens and the earth. Indeed, He is often-forgiving, most-merciful. (Al-Furqan [The Criterion] 25:5–6)

﴿وَلَقَدۡ نَعۡلَمُ أَنَّهُمۡ يَقُولُونَ إِنَّمَا يُعَلِّمُهُۥ بَشَرٞۗ لِّسَانُ ٱلَّذِي يُلۡحِدُونَ إِلَيۡهِ أَعۡجَمِيّٞ وَهَٰذَا
لِسَانٌ عَرَبِيّٞ مُّبِينٌ ١٠٣﴾

> We know indeed that they say: "It is a man that teaches him." The tongue they wickedly point to is

notably foreign, while this is Arabic, pure and clear. (An-Nahl [The Bees] 16:103)

It could not have been possible for a group of scholars to write such a magnificent book with such diverse ideas and information, morals, and ethics—let alone a single illiterate person. The Qur'an has challenged mankind to bring about such a book, and none has been able to do so throughout the centuries. This challenge still exists today. The authenticity of the Qur'an is in the Qur'an itself. Those who accuse Muhammad of writing it have not read the Qur'an nor studied the life of Muhammad and his noble character. He was a truthful, honest person and could not have forged a lie like this.

Muhammad Was a Man of War

Those who accused Muhammad stated that he fought many wars in order to expand his influence and dominate Arabia. They stated that after he immigrated to Medina, he was engaged in one battle after another and was not satisfied till he subdued all his enemies. They also stated that he drove the Jews out of their homes in Medina and Khaybar, killing many of them.

The permission to fight was given to the Muslims only in the second year after Hijra (immigration) to Medina. The Qur'an states that the Muslims were given permission in order to defend themselves against aggression and that they were forced out of their homes for no reason except that they held on to their faith.

﴿ أُذِنَ لِلَّذِينَ يُقَٰتَلُونَ بِأَنَّهُمْ ظُلِمُوا۟ ۚ وَإِنَّ ٱللَّهَ عَلَىٰ نَصْرِهِمْ لَقَدِيرٌ ﴿٣٩﴾ ٱلَّذِينَ أُخْرِجُوا۟ مِن
دِيَٰرِهِم بِغَيْرِ حَقٍّ إِلَّآ أَن يَقُولُوا۟ رَبُّنَا ٱللَّهُ ۗ

> To those against whom war is made, permission (to fight) is given, because they are wronged; and indeed God is most powerful for their aid. Those who have been forced out from their homes, in defiance of right, for no reason except that they say: "Our Lord is God." (Al-Hajj [The Pilgrimage] 22:39–40)

The Qur'an states clearly that fighting is only allowed in the cause of God and to defend oneself and country from aggression. Wrongdoing and transgression are not allowed in the fighting.

﴿ وَقَٰتِلُوا۟ فِى سَبِيلِ ٱللَّهِ ٱلَّذِينَ يُقَٰتِلُونَكُمْ وَلَا تَعْتَدُوٓا۟ ۚ إِنَّ ٱللَّهَ لَا يُحِبُّ ٱلْمُعْتَدِينَ ﴿١٩٠﴾ ﴾

> Fight in the cause of God those who fight you, but do not transgress limits; for God loves not transgressors. (Al-Baqara [The Cow] 2:190)

All the prophet's battles were defensive in nature. In the Battle of Badr, the Muslims left Medina with no intention to fight; they were only after the rich caravan of the Quraish. But when the Quraish forced them to fight, they fought, though they were few in number and not armed properly. They defeated their enemy despite great odds.

In the Battle of Uhud, the Quraish and their allies came to attack Medina with a large army. The Muslims defended their city in the mountain of Uhud on the outskirts of Medina. Their initial victory turned into defeat when the archers disobeyed the prophet's orders.

In the Battle of Ahzab, Medina was under siege, and the Muslims were hungry and in great trouble. However, they had faith and persevered, and God came to their rescue.

The Muslims went to Mecca to perform pilgrimage, but the Quraish refused to let them perform this religious rite. After the truce was broken by the Quraish, the Muslims marched into Mecca and opened it without bloodshed. The prophet (PBUH) did not punish nor seek revenge from those who tortured the Muslims and abused them for thirteen years in Mecca. Rather, he forgave them because he wanted to bring people together and let them serve God.

The prophet sent his army to fight the Romans because they killed his emissaries and abused the Muslims. It was necessary to stand up and help those who were wronged in order to allow them to practice their faith without oppression. The Qur'an confirms the rationale for fighting to safeguard the liberty and freedom of the oppressed:

﴿ وَقَٰتِلُوهُمْ حَتَّىٰ لَا تَكُونَ فِتْنَةٌ وَيَكُونَ ٱلدِّينُ لِلَّهِ ۖ فَإِنِ ٱنتَهَوْا۟ فَلَا عُدْوَٰنَ إِلَّا عَلَى ٱلظَّٰلِمِينَ ﴿١٩٣﴾ ﴾

> And fight them on until there is no more persecution and the religion becomes God's. But if they cease, let there be no hostility except to those who practice oppression. (Al-Baqara [The Cow] 2:193)

The goal of the fight is not to gain more land or abuse or oppress others or deny them their freedom. Muslims are forbidden from forcing anyone to become a Muslim. Those who want to keep their faith are allowed to practice it according to their tradition. The prophet allowed the Christian delegation from Najran to pray in his mosque according to their own tradition. The Jews and Christians enjoyed freedom under Muslim rule. An example was Muslim Spain, where all three religions lived in peace. It was only after the Inquisition that both Jews and Muslims were persecuted by the church, and many were forced to leave to safeguard their faith.

Islam does not like war or the killing of innocent people. The prophet gave clear orders to his troops not to kill a child, a woman, an elderly person, or those not involved in the war. He also gave instructions not to burn crops or destroy buildings.

The Qur'an orders Muslims to safeguard places of worship—whether they were mosques or churches or synagogues or monasteries—because in all these places, God is glorified.

وَلَوْلَا دَفْعُ ٱللَّهِ ٱلنَّاسَ بَعْضَهُم بِبَعْضٍ لَّهُدِّمَتْ صَوَٰمِعُ وَبِيَعٌ وَصَلَوَٰتٌ وَمَسَٰجِدُ يُذْكَرُ فِيهَا ٱسْمُ
ٱللَّهِ كَثِيرًا

> Did not God check one set of people by means of another, there would surely have been destroyed monasteries, churches, synagogues and mosques, in which the name of God is commemorated often. (Al-Hajj [Pilgrimage] 22:40)

Muhammad Married Too Many Wives to Satisfy His Desires

Muhammad was married to only one woman when he was in the prime of his life. He married his first wife, Khadija, when he was twenty-five years old. She was fifteen years older than him, and he used to work for her in trade. She respected him and sought to marry him, and she was a widow. She was his only wife for twenty-five years till she died in the tenth year after he became God's messenger. The rule in Islam is to have only one wife.

After Khadija died there was a need for someone to take care of Muhammad's daughters, who were young and needed a mother; so he married Sawda, his second wife.

Abu Bakr was Muhammad's close friend and trusted advisor. The custom of the Arabs at that time was to cement relationships by marriage, so Muhammad married Aisha, the daughter of Abu Bakr. She was the only virgin that he married.

She learned from him; she knew the Qur'an and was a scholar. She related many of his sayings and was a great source of knowledge because she lived for many years after Muhammad died. People asked her about him and his life and character.

Muhammad married Hafsah, the daughter of Umar, the prophet's close friend and advisor, because her father was sad and worried about his daughter after her divorce. Muhammad also wanted to cement their relationship.

Muhammad married the widows of the men who died in the Battle of Badr and Uhud to set a precedent, so that Muslims would do the same and take care of the widows and children of martyrs. Muhammad married Zainab in order to correct a misconception and to state that Muslims can marry the divorced wives of their adopted sons. Muhammad married Safiyya, the widow of a Jewish worrior and the daughter of a Jewish leader in Khaybar, to reconcile the hearts of Jews and Muslims.

Therefore, there were political reasons for some of these marriages because Muhammad was head of state and had certain responsibilities to fulfill. Another reason for his marriages was social: to take care of widows and orphans or to bring people together.

Though Muhammad married some widows who had children before from their previous marriage, he had no children from them. His children all came from Khadija, his first wife. The only exception was his son Ibrahim (Abraham) from Marium (Mary), who died as an infant.

Muslims Worship Muhammad

Muslims do not worship Muhammad; they worship the *one* and *only* God: Allah. Muhammad is human. He was born, and he died like other prophets and messengers before him. God does not die; He is alive and will be forever after everyone else has passed away.

﴿ وَلَا تَدۡعُ مَعَ ٱللَّهِ إِلَٰهًا ءَاخَرَۘ لَآ إِلَٰهَ إِلَّا هُوَۚ كُلُّ شَيۡءٍ هَالِكٌ إِلَّا وَجۡهَهُۥۚ لَهُ ٱلۡحُكۡمُ وَإِلَيۡهِ
تُرۡجَعُونَ ﴿٨٨﴾ ﴾

> Call not besides God on another god, there is no god but He. Everything that exists will perish except His face. To Him belongs the command, and to Him you will be brought back. (Al-Qasas [The Stories] 28:88)

Muhammad is human, and the Qur'an stresses the human nature of Muhammad. He had no control or power except what God gave him. The prophet did not know the unseen.

﴿ قُل لَّآ أَقُولُ لَكُمۡ عِندِي خَزَآئِنُ ٱللَّهِ وَلَآ أَعۡلَمُ ٱلۡغَيۡبَ وَلَآ أَقُولُ لَكُمۡ إِنِّي مَلَكٌۖ إِنۡ أَتَّبِعُ إِلَّا مَا
يُوحَىٰٓ إِلَيَّۚ قُلۡ هَلۡ يَسۡتَوِي ٱلۡأَعۡمَىٰ وَٱلۡبَصِيرُۚ أَفَلَا تَتَفَكَّرُونَ ﴿٥٠﴾ ﴾

> Say: "I tell you not that with me are the treasures of God, nor do I know what is hidden, nor do I

> tell you that I am an angel. I but follow what is revealed to me." Say: "Can the blind be equal to the seeing?" Will you then not consider? (Al-An'am [The Cattle] 6:50)

To Muslims, Muhammad is God's messenger and prophet. He applied the message of God in his character and behavior and became an example to follow. Muslims obey the orders of Muhammad and follow his example. Muslims love and cherish Muhammad but do not worship him or glorify him. The prophet (PBUH) told his companions, "Do not glorify me, like the Christians glorify the son of Mary, but say: "God's messenger and servant."

CPSIA information can be obtained at www.ICGtesting.com
Printed in the USA
LVOW06s1221161115

462771LV00001B/2/P

9 781681 644646